W9-CCY-364

Classics in Literacy Education

Historical Perspectives for Today's Teachers

Richard D. Robinson

INTERNATIONAL
Reading
Association

800 Barksdale Road, PO Box 8139
Newark, Delaware 19714-8139, USA
www.reading.org

IRA BOARD OF DIRECTORS

Donna M. Ogle, National-Louis University, Evanston, Illinois, *President* • Jerry L. Johns, Northern Illinois University, DeKalb, Illinois, *President-Elect* • Lesley Mandel Morrow, Rutgers University, New Brunswick, New Jersey, *Vice President* • Gregg M. Kurek, Bridgman Public Schools, Bridgman, Michigan • Jeanne R. Paratore, Boston University, Boston, Massachusetts • Lori L. Rog, Regina Public Schools, Regina, Saskatchewan • Carol Minnick Santa, Montana Academy, Kalispell, Montana • Rebecca L. Olness, Kent Public Schools, Kent, Washington • Doris Walker-Dalhouse, Minnesota State University Moorhead, Moorhead, Minnesota • Patricia L. Anders, University of Arizona, Tucson, Arizona • Timothy V. Rasinski, Kent State University, Kent, Ohio • Ann-Sofie Selin, Cygnaeus School, Åbo, Finland • Alan E. Farstrup, Executive Director

The International Reading Association attempts, through its publications, to provide a forum for a wide spectrum of opinions on reading. This policy permits divergent viewpoints without implying the endorsement of the Association.

Director of Publications   Joan M. Irwin
Editorial Director, Books and Special Projects   Matthew W. Baker
Senior Editor, Books and Special Projects   Tori Mello Bachman
Permissions Editor   Janet S. Parrack
Production Editor   Shannon Benner
Assistant Editor   Corinne M. Mooney
Editorial Assistant   Tyanna L. Collins
Publications Manager   Beth Doughty
Production Department Manager   Iona Sauscermen
Supervisor, Electronic Publishing   Anette Schütz-Ruff
Senior Electronic Publishing Specialist   Cheryl J. Strum
Electronic Publishing Specialist   R. Lynn Harrison
Proofreader   Charlene M. Nichols

Project Editor   Janet S. Parrack

Credits begin on page vi which is considered an extension of the copyright page.

Copyright 2002 by the International Reading Association, Inc.
All rights reserved. No part of this publication may be reproduced or transmitted in any form or by any means, electronic or mechanical, including photocopy, or any information storage and retrieval system, without permission from the publisher.

Library of Congress Cataloging-in-Publication Data
Robinson, Richard David, 1940–
    Classics in literacy education : historical perspectives for today's teachers / Richard Robinson.
        p.   cm.
Includes bibliographical references.
    ISBN 0-87207-174-X (alk. paper)
1. Reading teachers—Biography.   2. Reading—History.   3. Reading teachers—Training of.   I. Title.
    LB1050.2 .R63 2001
    428.4'071—dc21

                                                                2001005969

This book is dedicated to the men and women
of the Reading Hall of Fame, who by their
dedication to excellence in the teaching of reading
have set a standard for all teachers.

CONTENTS

CREDITS

*T*hese publishers have generously given permission to use extended quotations from the following copyrighted works. Every effort has been made to contact copyright holders and publishers for permission to reprint. Any oversights that may have occurred will be rectified in future printings.

From "The Word is Psy'-cho-lin-guis'-tics" by A. Sterl Artley, *School and Community*. Copyright © 1979 by Missouri State Teachers Association. Reprinted with permission.

From "Oral-Language Growth and Reading Ability" and "Individual Differences and Reading Instruction" by A. Sterl Artley, *The Elementary School Journal*. Copyright © 1953 and 1981 by University of Chicago Press. Reprinted with permission.

From "Correction of Reading Difficulties," "Basal Readers," and "Specific Reading Needs" by Emmett A. Betts, *Visual Digest*. Copyright © 1941, 1941, and 1943 by the American Optometric Association. Reprinted with permission.

From "Introduction" by A. Taylor, *The Philobiblon* by Richard de Bury. Copyright © 1948 by Regents of the University of California; renewed 1976 by Archer Taylor. Reprinted with permission of University of California Press.

From "What Should We Teach in Reading" by Arthur Gates, *School and Community*. Copyright © 1951 by Missouri State Teachers Association. Reprinted with permission.

From *School and Society* by J. Dewey. Copyright © 1900 by University of Chicago Press. Reprinted with permission.

From "Nature of Mature Reading" by William S. Gray. In H.M. Robinson (Ed.), *Promoting Maximal Reading Growth Among Able Learners*. Copyright © 1954 by University of Chicago Press. Reprinted with permission.

From "Objectives for the New Reading Program" by William S. Gray. In H.M. Robinson (Ed.), *Evaluation of Reading*. Copyright © 1958 by University of Chicago Press. Reprinted with permission.

From *Why Pupils Fail in Reading* by Helen M. Robinson. Copyright ©1946 by University of Chicago Press. Reprinted with permission.

From *Controversial Issues in Reading and Promising Solutions* by Helen M. Robinson. Copyright ©1961 by University of Chicago Press. Reprinted with permission.

From *Corrective Reading in Classroom and Clinic* by H.M. Robinson. Copyright ©1953 by University of Chicago Press. Reprinted with permission.

From *Sequential Development of Reading Abilities* by H.M. Robinson. Copyright ©1960 by University of Chicago Press. Reprinted with permission.

From *Diagnosing and Correcting Reading Disabilities* (2nd ed.) by George D. Spache. Copyright ©1981 by Allyn & Bacon. Reprinted with permission.

From *Investigating the Issues of Reading Disabilities* by George D. Spache. Copyright ©1976 by Allyn & Bacon. Reprinted with permission.

From "Reading as Communication" by David Russell, *Childhood Education*. Copyright ©1951 by Association for Childhood Education. Reprinted with permission.

From "Reading and Healthy Personality" by David H. Russell, *Elementary English*. Copyright ©1952 by National Council of Teachers of English. Reprinted with permission.

FOREWORD

*I*t seems that our world has now become focused on standards and outcomes designed to professionalize our daily endeavors. More so than ever, we are left with the message from politicians and policy makers that we in the reading field are somewhat less than professional. And for whatever reason, we tend to meekly accept the chastisement and strive to do what we have always done so well, but now with neatly prescribed standards and outcomes that move us ever closer and closer to a one-size-fits-all national literacy curriculum. And so, we believe ourselves to be professionals. If only we recognized, valued, and embraced the history of our field, we would be taking the first step to becoming a true profession.

If we genuinely appreciated the contributions of those who have gone before, we truly would understand that we have a rich and valued history, if not a common ground to build on for our profession's future and the futures of learners throughout this uncertain world. Yet in our field's *Standards for Reading Professionals*, there is but a single standard focusing only partially on our heritage. Even then, only the reading coordinator and the teacher educator are expected to have a comprehensive understanding of the importance of and contributions to the knowledge base provided by the researchers and scholars of the past century. Only the lowest levels of knowledge or awareness are expected of classroom professionals. Reading specialists are expected to hold but a basic understanding of our professional forebearers. Hence, is it any surprise that so many individuals in the field regularly fall sway to the fads and the hucksterisms that have been debunked so often in the past? Is it any surprise that some might logically argue that we are doomed to fight the phonics wars again and again in the future because we have not learned from our past? If all the world is a play, then it is history that both critiques our past performance and foreshadows our future. It is through knowledge of the history of reading pedagogy that we will learn to become a true profession.

And so, to such a drama enters *Classics in Literacy Education: Historical Perspectives for Today's Teachers* by Richard Robinson. Long an observer of our profession's ever expanding theory, research, and concepts of best practice, Dr. Robinson is a member of that professional generation that last had direct contact with the founders of the field of modern reading pedagogy. Hence, it is neither surprising nor ill timed that a book such as *Classics in Literacy Education* appears as we struggle through these troubled beginnings of the new century.

With *Classics in Literacy Education*, we have touchstones to our professional roots. We have the opportunity to read important vignettes on professional themes that will always be on our research agendas and influencing our daily practice. As we read the works of our academic progenitors in this book, such as William S. Gray, Arthur I. Gates, David H. Russell, Helen M. Robinson, and Nila Banton Smith among others, we see that there is much truth in the statement, "All that is old is new once again." Although we as reading educators may not truly reinvent the wheel on a regular basis, it is obvious that our design work as observed in our best journals and yearbooks or our technical monographs and methods books rarely gives more than lip service to the foundational studies and writings of our past. Related literature sections are considered outdated if references are over a decade old. As we forever look forward to the brave new world, we overlook the wisdom of those who have come before. The wisdom of the past leaders noted in this book seems in so many cases lost to the times.

Such a practice may exist more out of ignorance than professional malice. Yet the results are the same—professional myopia. *Classics in Literacy Education* takes us in the right direction, opening up the wisdom and knowledge of the giants in the field in a form to be used by individuals seeking to provide literacy training to students across the lifespan, as well as to those desiring to expand the boundaries of knowledge through the generation of new theories and research. *Classics in Literacy Education* gives readers the opportunity to read the actual words of important figures on forever-important topics. Indeed, there is no individual in the professional community that cannot benefit from careful review of the writings contained in this source. In fact, one might postulate that individuals will benefit best by reviewing this text multiple times as they advance through professional developmental levels over the years. And of course, it would be hoped that readers will ponder Robinson's well-considered reflective questions in order to integrate historic thoughts into modern theory and research, and then follow his recommendations for further readings to review both historical works and primary sources.

The publication of this book by the International Reading Association provides all members of the field an opportunity to celebrate as it continues what we hope will be an ongoing series of publications relating to our historical roots. It is time for the members of the field to clearly demonstrate an appreciation of history and an ability to learn from history. With such a degree of maturity, we might rightfully call ourselves members of a profession. Reading, evaluating, and valuing the timeless wisdom of our forebearers included in *Classics in Literacy Education* takes us in the right direction.

Norman A. Stahl
Northern Illinois University
DeKalb, Illinois, USA

INTRODUCTION

If we see further today, it is simply because we stand on the shoulders of giants.

—Isaac Newton

*T*he field of reading education has a rich, renowned, and largely forgotten history. From earliest times, educators have thought and written with skill and insight about the teaching of reading and have confronted its myriad facets and mysteries. Educators of the past have struggled and reflected deeply about many of the same dilemmas and problems faced by reading teachers of today. Because of this shared ground, we need to listen carefully to reading educators of the past.

Mark Twain defined a classic as a book "which everyone wants to read but no one actually does!" For many teachers, "educational classic" brings to mind a book or other writing that is characteristically remote, difficult to understand, and of little relevance to current teaching practices. A classic by definition, however, simply means a frequently referenced work in which many readers throughout the years have found insight. Moreover, even a cursory exploration of classic books and articles reveals that their authors typically reached conclusions that have been confirmed, not refuted, by subsequent research and actual classroom practice.

Teachers Should Know Reading's Past History

There are a number of reasons why awareness of the classic writers from reading's rich historical past is important to today's teachers. Often we are restricted to a parochial view of reading instruction when we limit our opportunity to experience the in-depth understanding and knowledge of these classic writers. Unfortunately, in today's educational world, we are influenced heavily by fads and foibles in reading education. Ideally, the classics in reading education should become a solid foundation or benchmark from which current reading teachers can experiment with ideas and practices, clearly knowing they have a reliable basis for determining the effectiveness of these new ventures.

The most critical reason for an understanding of reading's history is simply that many of the classic writers saw and understood the reading process with great individual insight and understanding. Rather than being of only passing historical interest, these classic readings are relevant and important for today's reading teacher. They have clearly stood the test of time and, because of their enduring quality, contain much to inspire current teachers to address the most fundamental beliefs and practices in reading education.

The Purpose of This Book

A word of caution as you begin your consideration of the classics in the field of reading education: If you expect to find the "perfect approach" or easy answers to the teaching of reading, you will not find it here. Rather than presenting a quick fix, the writers highlighted in this collection presupposed a reader who is willing to reflect, reread, and meditate on their words. They make no promise of definitive answers and solutions—only a deepened insight into the questions and problems.

This is not a history book in the sense that it traces the development of reading education from its origins through current practice. Rather it is an attempt to let reading teachers of the past speak to contemporary educators about issues and concerns of common interest. The result is that, despite differences in time and teaching methods, there is still much of value that can be shared among all teachers of reading.

The readings included were chosen using a variety of criteria. The primary factor was a selection's relevance for today's classroom reading teacher: Does the material address the problems and issues facing contemporary literacy programs? Are answers and suggestions provided that will stimulate teachers to reevaluate their current teaching practices and encourage positive change? Different readings might remind teachers of the battles already fought over various reading philosophies and approaches, and based on this knowledge, prepare them to make appropriate decisions about their reading instruction. In other words, what is thought of as "new" and "innovative" today might in reality be a well-established literacy technique or concept of yesterday. Other readings are included here simply because of the obvious joy and delight the authors expressed about their experiences with reading.

During the selection process, I was aware that the history of reading has not always been clear and seamless, without diversions and disagreements. Issues such as handedness and learning to read, eye movements and reading disability, and the role of typography and reading success were of prominent concern to past reading educators. Today, these issues are of great interest to the reading historian but have little relevance for reading teachers.

Perhaps the most difficult task in preparing this book was choosing which classic authors to include. Reading has been a mainstay of education and of great interest and concern to educators through the ages, and this significance is reflected in the vast library of resources and writings on the topic. To guide the final selection process, I looked at amount and quality of writings, as well as relevance for today's reading teacher, and I tried to include as wide a variety of literacy topics as possible. Finally, and somewhat arbitrarily, I decided not to include any living authors. Also, it is interesting to note the number of authors included who happen to be members of the Reading Hall of Fame. Although this was not a criterion for selection, it reflects the high esteem in which these authors were held by their peers.

Organization of the Chapters

The authors are arranged in this book according to their year of birth, and they are introduced with a brief overview of their professional lives. Included are references to their teaching backgrounds, primary areas of research, and their most noted professional publications. Following the introductions are selections from the author's writings on a variety of topics. For those interested in learning more about each reading authority, an annotated list of materials, written either about or by the author, follows the excerpts

At the end of each chapter are "Reflections," designed to encourage readers to ruminate on their teaching practices, especially in relation to the views and ideas of these reading pioneers. In some cases, the material will reinforce present practices, although in others it may challenge and encourage rethinking on a particular reading issue. In either instance, the primary goal is for teachers to become well grounded in practices and beliefs about reading through knowledge of the rich historical legacy of this field.

Historical Beliefs About Reading

Consider the following statements about reading, which have been selected from a variety of authors, some well known and some of lesser note. Each quote conveys the thoughts and feelings of former reading educators, making them true colleagues of today's teachers. We need to respect them for the deep insights they brought to the field of reading and for how those insights affect us in the modern world.

> When a child can talk, 'tis time he should learn to read. And when he reads, put into his hands some very pleasant book suited to his capacity, wherein the entertainment he finds may draw him on, and reward his pains in reading. Aesop's fables with pictures may be made use of to this purpose. Talk often to him about the stories he has read, and hear him tell them. This will bring delight in reading and to express himself handsomely. (Waugh, 1752, pp. 11–12)

> Reading or language is the outward representation of the mind.... (Warblis, 1646, p. 1)

> And indeed how many volumes of learning whatever a man possesses, he is still deplorably poor in his understanding till he has made those several parts of learning his own property by reading and reasoning, by judging for himself, and remembering what he has read. (Watts, 1811, p. 54)

> What more pleasing variety can there be, then that of children's dispositions and fantasies? What better recreation than to read and discourse on so many sundry subjects we meet with in ordinary authors? Besides, the delight which is to be taken by our scholars' ready progress in a current way will far exceed all care and toyle [toil] that can be bestowed in helping them to profit. (Hoole, 1660, p. viii)

> To teach reading as mere combination of words which do not teach anything, which are often unintelligible to young persons and which leave minds in states of listless curiosity and total ignorance is a waste of time. (Blair, 1806, p. 10)

> [T]here may be several difficulties in it [a reading selection] which we cannot easily understand and conquer at the first reading, for want of a

fuller comprehension of the author's whole scheme. And therefore in such treatises, we should not stay till we master every difficulty at the first perusal; for perhaps, many of these would appear to be solved when we have proceeded further in that book, or would vanish of themselves upon a second reading. (Watts, 1811, p. 43)

I observe that betwixt three and four years of age a child hath great propensity to peep into a book, and then is the most reasonable time (if convenience may be had otherwise) for him to begin to learn. But acquaint him a little with the matter beforehand, for that will entice him to read it, and make him more observant of what he reads. After he hath read, ask him such general questions out of the story, as are most easy for him to answer, and he will better remember it. (Hoole, 1659, pp. 2, 22)

It is certain that many become authors before they become Readers. (Steele, 1714, p. 279)

A Reader that has any Understanding is naturally a Commentator. (Steele, 1714, p. 319)

Reading is that means or method of knowledge whereby we acquaint ourselves with what other men have written, or published to the world in their writings. These arts of reading and writing are of infinite advantage, for by them we are made partakers of the sentiments, observations, reasonings, and improvements of all the learned world, in the most remote nations, and in former ages almost from the beginning of mankind. (Watts, 1811, p. 21)

Finally, I offer a personal observation concerning the development and writing of this book. I tried to read and review as many of each author's writings as possible. Although I was removed in time and location, I began to see these individuals as friends and fellow reading educators. Each in their own way seemed to have experienced similar problems and successes to my own in the teaching of reading. It is my hope that readers of this book will share this experience.

REFERENCES

Blair, D. (1806). *The class book: Or three hundred and sixty-five reading lessons adapted to the use of schools for every day in the year.* London: R. Taylor.

Hoole, C. (1660). *A new discovery of the old art of teaching school in four small treatises.* London: Printed by F.T. for Andrew Crook at the Green Dragon in Pauls Church-yard.

Steele, R. (1714). *The reader*. London: F. Toufon.

Warblis, S. (1646). *A common writing: Whereby two, although not understanding one of the others language, yet by the helps thereof, may communicate their minds one to another*. London: n. p.

Watts, I. (1811). *The improvement of the mind*. London: F.C. & J. Rivington.

Waugh, J. (1752). *Education of children and young students in all its branches with a short catalogue of the best book in polite learning and the sciences*. London: J. Waught.

In books find the dead as if they were alive.

Books delight us when prosperity smiles upon us; they comfort us inseparably when stormy fortune frowns on us.

All the glory of the world would be buried in oblivion, unless God had provided mortals the remedy of books.

Whosoever therefore acknowledges himself to be a zealous follower of truth, of happiness, of wisdom, of science, or even of faith, must of necessity make himself a lover of books.

Richard de Bury (1287–1345)

*A*lthough more than 6 centuries have passed since Richard de Bury wrote "The Philobiblon" [The Love of Books], this remarkable essay on the reading experience still speaks to readers today. In de Bury's words we truly see the thoughts of a man who felt reading was one of life's most important and enjoyable activities. Written near the end of de Bury's life, "The Philobiblon" was widely read and appreciated by readers throughout the Middle Ages.

Richard de Bury spent his life as a governmental official in the royal court of England. His primary responsibilities included a wide variety of important diplomatic and domestic duties. Through these activities, de Bury was able to build what was considered then the premier private library of his generation. Although no lists of titles of what he owned now exist, comments from contemporary writers of his time suggest the vastness of de Bury's manuscript collection. They noted that he maintained a library in each of his residences, and that it was nearly impossible to stand or move about without stepping on his many references. "The Philobiblon" is one of the first writings about reading and is still considered one of the best on the love of reading.

It may seem unusual to begin a book on the writings of prominent reading teachers with those of a noneducator, but Richard de Bury has much to say to the modern educator about the joys of reading. His writing shows an individual who thought deeply and emotionally about reading, and therefore, I thought he deserved to be included.

Excerpts From the Writing of Richard de Bury

Reasons for Reading

In the following passages, de Bury describes his personal reasons for reading (Thomas, 1966). Note how a love for reading tends to change a reader in various ways.

> *The desirable treasure of wisdom and science [the reading of*
> *books], which all men desire by an instinct of nature, infinitely*
> *surpasses all the riches of the world; in respect of which*
> *precious stones are worthless; in comparison with which silver*
> *is as clay and pure gold is as a little sand; at whose splendor the*

sun and moon are dark to look upon; compared with whose marvelous sweetness honey and manna are bitter to the taste. O value of wisdom that fadeth not away with time, virtue ever flourishing, that cleanseth its possessor from all venom! (p. 7)

In books I find the dead as if they were alive; in books I foresee things to come; in books warlike affairs are set forth; from books come forth the laws of peace. All things are corrupted and decay in time...all the glory of the world would be buried in oblivion, unless God had provided mortals with the remedy of reading. Alexander, the conqueror of the earth, Julius, the invader of Rome and of the world, who, the first in war and arts, assumed universal empire under his single rule, Fabricius and stern Cato would now have been unknown to fame, if the aid of books had been wanting. Towers have been razed to the ground; cities have been overthrown; triumphal arches have perished from decay; nor can either pope or king find any means of more easily conferring the privilege of perpetuity than by books. The book that he has made renders its author this service in return, that so long as the book survives its author remains immortal and cannot die.... (pp. 9–10)

For the meaning of the voice perishes with the sound; truth lying in the mind is wisdom that is hid and treasure that is seen; but truth which shines forth in books desires to manifest itself to every impressionable sense. It commends itself to the sight when it is read, to the hearing when it is heard, and moreover in a manner to the touch, when it suffers itself to be transcribed, bound, corrected and observed. (pp. 10–11)

But the written truth of books, not transient but permanent, plainly offers itself to be observed, and by means of the previous spheres of the eyes, passing through the vestibule of perception and the courts of imagination, enters the chamber of the intellect, taking its place in the courts of memory, where it engenders the eternal truth of the mind. Finally, we must consider what pleasantness of teaching there is in books, how easy, how secret! How safely we lay bare the poverty of human ignorance to books without feeling any shame! They are masters who instruct us without rod or ferule, without angry words, without clothes or money. If you come to them they are not asleep; if you ask and inquire of them they do not withdraw themselves; they do not chide if you make mistakes; they do not laugh at you if you are ignorant. O books, who alone are liberal and free, who give to all who ask of you and enfranchise all who serve you faithfully. (pp. 11–12)

Moreover, since books are the aptest teachers...it is fitting to bestow them the honour and the affection that we owe to our teachers...since all men naturally desire to know, and since by means of books we can attain the knowledge of the ancients, which is to be desired beyond all riches, what man living according to nature would not feel the desire of books? And although we know that swine trample pearls under foot, the wise man will not therefore be deterred from gathering the pearls that lie before him. A library of wisdom, then, is more precious than all wealth and all things that are desirable cannot be compared to it. Whoever therefore claims to be zealous of truth, of happiness, of wisdom or knowledge, aye, even of the faith, must become a lover of books. (pp. 17–18)

Besides all this, we were frequently made ambassador of this most illustrious Prince of everlasting memory, and were sent on the most various affairs of state, now to the Holy See, now to the Court of France, and again to various powers of the world, on tedious embassies and in times of danger, always carrying with us, however, that love of books which many waters could not quench. For this like a delicious draught sweetened the bitterness of our journeys and after the perplexing intricacies and troublesome difficulties of causes, and the all but inextricable labyrinths of public affairs afforded us a little breathing space to enjoy a balmier atmosphere. (p. 56)

The Price of Books

For those of us today who despair at finding adequate funds to pay for all the books we would like to own, it is interesting to realize this is not a new dilemma.

[N]amely, that no dearness of price ought to hinder a man from the buying of books.... For if it is wisdom only that makes the price of books, which is an infinite treasure to mankind, and if the value of books is unspeakable, as the premises show, how shall the bargain be shown to be dear where an infinite good is being brought? (p. 19)

[No] man can serve both books and Mammon. (p. 93)

Collecting Books

In the following passage (Thomas, 1966), de Bury clearly describes what it means to be an avid book collector, especially in the encouragement of friends to donate to one's collection.

There flowed in, instead of presents and guerdons [rewards], and instead of gifts and jewels, soiled tracts and battered codices pleasant to our eye and ear. Then the aumbries [libraries] of the most famous monasteries were thrown open, cases were unlocked and caskets were undone, and volumes that had slumbered through long ages in their tombs wake up and are astonished, and those that had lain hidden in dark places are bathed in the ray of unwonted light. These long lifeless books, once most dainty, but now become corrupt and loathsome, covered with litters of mice and pierced with the gnawings of the worms, and who were once clothed in purple and fine linen, now lying in sackcloth and ashes, given up to oblivion, seemed to have become habitations of the moth. Natheless [nevertheless] among these, seizing the opportunity, we would sit down with more delight than a fastidious physician among his stores of gums and spices, and there we found the object and the stimulus of our affections. Thus the sacred vessels of learning came into our control and stewardship; some by gift, others by purchase, and some lent to us for a reason.

No wonder that when people saw that we were contented with gifts of this kind, they were anxious of their own accord to minister to our needs with those things that they were more

*willing to dispense with than the things they secured by
ministering to our service.... Indeed, if we had loved gold and
silver goblets, high-bred horses, or no small sums of money, we
might in those days have furnished forth a rich treasury. But in
truth we wanted manuscripts not moneyscripts; we loved
codices more than florins, and preferred slender pamphlets to
pampered palfreys [saddlehorses]. (pp. 54–56)*

Benefits of Reading

In a short passage, de Bury describes the enormous rewards of reading, in terms of gaining both a wide knowledge of the world and individual personal growth (Taylor, 1948).

*The arts and sciences, the benefits of which no mind is
sufficient to tell, depends upon books. How highly must we
reckon their marvelous power, since by means of them we view
the boundaries of the world and of time and, as in a mirror of
eternity, behold the things that are not as those that are! In
books we scale the mountains; we search the deep gulfs of the
abysses; we behold the finny tribes which the common air can
in no way contain alive. We distinguish the properties of
streams and springs of different lands, and out of books we dig
the various kinds of metals and of gems, and the ore of every
mineral. We learn the virtues of plants and trees and shrubs
and view at will all the progeny [offspring] of Neptune, of Cere,
and Pluto. And if it delight us to visit the inhabitants of heaven,
betaking ourselves to Taurus, Caucasus, or Olympus, we pass
beyond the realms of Juno and measure out the sevenfold
territory of the planets with curves and circles. At last we behold
the lofty firmament on high, pictured in endless variety with
signs and degrees and figures. There we look upon the Antarctic
Pole, whose turning neither eye has seen nor ear heard, and
behold with delectable joy the shining Milky Way, and the
Zodiac pictured with celestial animals. Passing thence, we cross
by means of books to the separate substances, that the intellect
may salute its kindred intelligences and behold with the eye of*

the spirit the First Cause of all things, the Unmoved Mover of infinite power, and be filled with love without end. Lo! By the aid of books we attain the reward of our final happiness while we are yet pilgrims. And what more? Assuredly, as we have learned from the teaching of Deneca, indolence without letters is death and the burial of the living man. And so, arguing from the opposite, we conclude that occupation with letters of books is the life of man. (pp. 83–84)

Books delight us, when prosperity smiles upon us; they comfort us inseparably when storm fortune frowns on us. They lend validity to human compacts, and no serious judgments are made without their help. (Thomas, 1966, p. 94)

Care of Books

What teacher has not seen his or her own students' behavior in this vivid description of how books are mishandled or abused?

First, then, let there be considerate moderation in the opening and shutting of books, that they be not opened in headlong haste nor, when our inspection is ended, be thrown away without being duly closed. For we ought to care far more diligently for a book than a boot.

But the race of scholars [students] is commonly educated badly and, unless it be curbed by the rules of its elders, becomes accustomed to childishness. They are moved by irritable temperament; they swell with impertinence; they give judgment as though certain of everything, whereas they are expert in nothing.

You shall chance to see some stiff-necked youth sluggishly seating himself for study, and while the frost is sharp in the winter time, his nose, all watery with the biting cold, begins to drip. Nor does he condescend to wipe it with his cloth until he has wet the books spread out before him with vile dew. Would that such a one were given in place of a book a cobbler's apron! He has a nail almost as black as jet and reeking with foul filth, *and with this he marks the place of any matter that pleaseth him. He sorts out innumerable straws which he sets in different places, evidently that the mark may bring back to him what his memory cannot hold. These straws, because the stomach of the book does not digest them and no one takes them out, at first distend it beyond its normal place of closing and at length, being quite overlooked, begin to rot. He halts not at eating fruits and cheese over the open page and, in a slovenly way, shifts his cup hither and thither. And because he has not his alms bag at hand, he casts the residue of the fragments into the book.... Soon doubling his elbows, he reclines upon the book and by his short study invites a long sleep and, by spreading out the wrinkles, bends the margins of the leaves, doing no small harm to the volume.*

Especially, moreover, must we restrain impudent youths from handling books—those youth who, when they have learned to draw the shapes of the letters, soon begin, if opportunity be granted them, to be uncouth scribblers on the best volumes and, where they see some larger margin about the text, make a show with monstrous letters; and if any other triviality whatsoever occurs to their imagination, their unchastened pen hastens at once to draw it out. There the Latinist and the sophister and every unlearned scribe proves the goodness of his pen, a practice which we have seen to be too often injurious to the best of books, both as concerns their usefulness and their price.

There are also certain thieves who make terrible havoc by cutting off the margins [of books] for paper on which to write their letters, leaving only the written text; or they turn to various abuses the flyleaves which are bound in for the protection of the book. This sort of sacrilege ought to be punished under pain of anathema [excommunication]. (Taylor, 1948, pp. 93–95)

REFERENCES

Taylor, A. (1948). *The Philobiblon*. Berkeley and Los Angeles: University of California.

Thomas, E.C. (1966). *The love of books: The Philobiblon of Richard de Bury*. New York: Cooper Square.

Reflections

If you found these excerpts from "The Philobiblon" of interest, consider reading the entire text, which reads like a personal conversation with a friend about the many joys found in a life of reading. The following are suggestions as to how you might incorporate some of the ideals from "The Philobiblon" into your own personal reading experiences, as well as your classroom literacy program:

1. The most important goal of reading instruction is to encourage "a love for reading." What reasons does Richard de Bury suggest for reading? How can you encourage students to see reading as an important part of their lives?

2. What are the most important benefits of reading you have discovered? Consider how you might share your experiences as a reader with your students.

FURTHER READING

Henrickson, G.L. (1929). Ancient reading. *The Classical Journal, 25*, 182–186.
    This is a historical description of reading in antiquity, centering on the Greek and Roman empires. It is an important resource for those studying the early history of reading and writing.

Manguel, A. (1996). *A history of reading*. New York: Viking.
    This is a personal history of Manguel's many and varied encounters with print, which he uses as an introduction to the study of the history of reading.

Matthews, M.M. (1966). *Teaching to read: Historically considered*. Chicago: University of Chicago Press.
    This is an important reference in the study of the history of literacy education. The author traces language development from earliest times through the present.

The primary purpose of reading in school is to extend the experiences of boys and girls, to stimulate their thinking powers, and to elevate their tastes. The ultimate end of instruction in reading is to enable the reader to participate intelligently in the thought life of the world and appreciatively in its recreational activities. This objective emphasizes the importance of the content of what is read and attaches new significance to it.

We need in elementary and secondary schools today inspiring teachers of broad interests who will share with their pupils the pleasures derived from the reading of good literature. They should also recognize fully their obligation to devote much time and attention to the problem of broadening the reading interests of their pupils and improving their tastes.

[O]ne of the greatest needs in American education today [1949] is to teach boys and girls to react intelligently to all that they see, to all they hear, and to all they read.

William S. Gray (1885–1960)

*W*illiam S. Gray can be considered the premier reading educator of the first half of the 20th century. In a long and distinguished career in education, he served as a rural elementary school teacher and principal, as well as a faculty member and Dean of Education at the University of Chicago (Chicago, Illinois, USA).

Gray wrote more than 500 books, articles, and research reports dealing with the field of literacy education. Among the most notable of these publications are *The Academic and Professional Preparation of Secondary-School Teachers* (1935), *On Their Own in Reading* (1948), *Classroom Techniques in Improving Reading* (1949), and *The Teaching of Reading and Writing* (1956 report of a worldwide study for UNESCO). Gray was the first to organize a continuing series of reports that summarized and synthesized the then existing knowledge in reading. While at the University of Chicago, he was instrumental in the establishment of a yearly conference on reading. These meetings and the subsequent annual yearbooks, which he edited from 1938 to 1952, are some of the most important references in the history of reading education. Gray was also the chairman of the yearbook committees of the National Society for the Study of Education's influential reports on reading in 1927, 1937, and 1948. It was also during his tenure at the University of Chicago that Gray was responsible for the development of one of the first formal teacher training courses in reading education.

Gray was a coauthor of the Basic Reading Series and Elson-Gray Readers, which were forerunners of the more widely known "Dick and Jane" basic readers published by Scott, Foresman. He was one of the founders of the International Reading Association (1956), and served as president of the American Educational Research Association (1932–1933). Gray also made significant contributions to reading research and literature about the diagnosis and correction of reading difficulties. In 1915, the first edition of the "Gray Oral Reading Test" was published, which was to shape assessment procedures in literacy education for many years. As the title indicates, reading was evaluated orally rather than in the more traditional format of silent reading followed by a written examination. During this time, Gray published *Remedial Cases in Reading: Their Diagnosis and Treatment* (1922), a landmark study that for the first time described students' reading problems in detail, emphasizing causation and suggesting appropriate remedial treatment.

It is difficult to summarize entirely the professional activities of William S. Gray as the vast scope of his research and writing is without equal in the field of reading education. His work identifies a reading philosophy that was eclectic in nature and based on the fundamental belief in the importance of the well-trained classroom teacher as the center of an effective reading program. Perhaps his lifetime of work in the field of reading was summarized best by Arthur Gates (1960/1961): "Dr. Gray labored to improve the teaching of reading for a longer period of time [more than half a century] with a greater singleness of purpose and in a wider variety of enterprises than anyone else in history."

Excerpts From the Writing of William S. Gray

William S. Gray was a strong advocate of the educational philosophy of John Dewey. In the following excerpts, Gray (1925) describes his own beliefs as to the fundamental reasons for the teaching of reading, and quotes Dewey in his comments about the influences of society on the school reading program, particularly in relation to establishing goals for instruction.

Point of View

Justification of any subject in the curriculum is that it enables pupils to engage effectively in desirable life activities. In keeping with this principle, instruction in reading should take account first of the reading experiences of children and adults in the home, in school, and in all social life. Information about these experiences aids in determining the kinds of reading that people do and should learn to do better. It may also reveal the reading activities that deserve and need special encouragement.

Relation of Reading to School Activities

The most important change of recent years in classroom instruction is the enrichment of the course of study and of the opportunities offered to children. Instead of a few textbooks relating to a limited number of topics, the progressive school today provides wide reading opportunities in many fields. Furthermore, the solution of most classroom problems requires the skillful use of books and sources of information. The library "is the place where the children bring the experiences, the problems, the questions, the particular facts which they have found and discuss them so that new light may be thrown upon them, particularly new light from the experiences of others." (Dewey, 1900, p. 100)

These tendencies have resulted in establishing a very close relationship between reading and practically every school activity. As a special subject of instruction, it is intimately related to children's daily experiences and language activities, and should be taught in connection with them. As a means of gaining information and pleasure, it is essential in every content subject, such as history, geography, arithmetic, science, and literature. In fact, rapid progress in these subjects depends in a large degree on the ability of pupils to read independently and intelligently. It follows that good teaching must provide for the improvement and refinement of the reading attitudes, habits, and skills that are needed in all school activities involving reading. (Gray, 1925, pp. 1–2)

A Definition of a Mature Reader

An important consideration in any reading program is to adequately determine the type of readers we want to develop based on our teaching efforts. In the following passage, Gray (1954) summarizes the work of a number of classroom teachers, reading specialists, and university faculty concerning the definition of a mature reader. This statement was selected because of its clarity and importance for today's teachers of reading.

[T]he competent, or mature reader, exhibits the following attainments:

1. He perceives words quickly, accurately, and independently. He has acquired the understandings, attitudes, and skills involved in recognizing both meanings and pronunciations and is able to make efficient application of the skills as needed.

2. *He secures a clear grasp of the meaning of what he reads. This includes not only a recognition of the literal meaning of passages but also the sensing of implied meanings and ability to make generalizations and to reach conclusions on the basis of the facts presented. At each step in this process the mature reader makes use of all that he knows or can find out that helps to clarify and enrich the meaning of the passages read.*

3. *He reacts thoughtfully to what he reads. He adopts an inquiring attitude toward such items as the completeness, relevance, and accuracy of the information presented; the adequacy of the author's treatment of a topic; the validity of the generalizations presented; and, at times, the rhetorical effectiveness and the literacy quality of the material read. In reaching conclusions concerning such matters, the mature reader makes use of objective criteria or applies rational standards of judgment. As a result of this total process he acquires not only an intellectual grasp of the material read but an emotional apprehension of its value and significance.*

4. *As the foregoing processes occur, the efficient reader integrates the ideas acquired through reading with previous experiences so that wrong concepts are corrected, new insights are acquired, broader interest and rational attitudes are developed, and a richer and more stable personality is acquired. The fact was emphasized...that, unless a reader is highly efficient in all four aspects of interpretation, he is more or less ineffective and immature. (p. 12)*

Goals of an Effective Reading Program

In 1958, Gray identified and discussed four major areas that he believed should be primary goals of all reading programs. Despite the fact that he wrote this almost 50 years ago, the goals remain relevant for today's reading teacher:

1. *To promote a growing understanding and deep appreciation of the distinctive role and values of reading in an age of mass media. Some of the specific goals sought are: a clear recognition of the possibilities of a rich, meaningful life through the intelligent choice and use of reading and other aids to information, learning, and pleasure; a knowledge of the most effective ways in which reading and other mass media can be used cooperatively, or separately, in securing needed information, in solving problems, and in securing wholesome pleasure; and wide acquaintance with the best sources to consult in keeping posted on the output of each medium, including critical reviews of books, motion pictures, and radio and television programs. Such an orientation is essential if children are to adopt right attitudes toward reading and make intelligent choices.*

2. *To extend and enrich experience through reading and to promote increasing participation in the thought-life of the world in harmony with the background, learning capacity, and level of maturity of the pupils taught. Specific goals sought are: clear understanding and intelligent adjustment to one's immediate environment— social, natural, physical, civic; penetrating insight into the distinctive characteristics of our times—their technological aspects, the world environment of which we are an integral part, and the needs, aspirations, and conflicting views of different national and cultural groups; the thorough, orderly mastery of the basic facts, principles, and disciplines inherent in each essential area of the curriculum; and a growing acquaintance with our cultural heritage. The understandings thus provided not only promote ability to adjust effectively to the needs of contemporary life, but provide an indispensable*

background for clear understanding and interpretation in subsequent reading activities.

3. *To cultivate interests in personal reading that will illuminate, direct, and inspire the present and future life of all readers. This involves helping them in various school activities to identify compelling motives for reading; revealing in various convincing ways the gratifying rewards inherent in well-chosen books and selections—their intriguing and challenging content, the better understanding provided of self, people, and life in different times and places, the challenging questions posed, new areas to explore, and the use of words and forms of expression that give life and vitality to what is read; providing an environment of attractive books of varying content and range in difficulty; promoting keen discrimination in the choice of materials; with the co-operation of parents, helping children develop daily schedules which provide time for study and personal reading at home; and reserving frequent periods in which children may share their reading experiences and identify new areas that will provide thrilling adventures through reading.*

4. *To promote continuous progress toward the high level of competence in reading that current life demands. The evidence now available suggests that a minimum standard of twelfth-grade reading ability is essential for all who are capable of achieving it. The specific goals sought are: the accurate, independent, and instantaneous perception of words; a clear, accurate grasp of the literal meaning of a passage, including the recognition of the kind of material read and the author's purpose, the fusing of separate meanings into the ideas intended, the arousal of appropriate mental imagery, and a clear recognition of important points, key concepts, the patterns of expression used, and the author's organization of the ideas presented; the enrichment of the literal meaning of what*

*is read by the recognition of implied meanings, the recall
of all one knows or can find out that contributes to a
fuller understanding of the passage, and the recognition
of the conclusions and generalizations justified by the
content of the passage; thoughtful evaluation of what is
read, including both critical reactions and appreciative
responses; fusing, combining, or integrating the ideas
acquired with previous experiences so that new or clearer
understandings, rational attitudes, and improved
patterns of thinking and behaving are acquired (this is
the heart of the learning act in reading); and utilizing the
various attitudes and skills described above as they are
needed in achieving various ends to be attained. (Gray,
1958, pp. 12–13)*

Enjoyment of Good Literature

The use of a wide variety of reading materials has always been considered to be an important part of all effective classroom reading programs. In the following passage, Gray (1931) describes in detail why he believed in this tenet of reading instruction.

*[A]n improved program of teaching provides for the orderly
development of desirable reading attitudes and habits during
the reading period, for wide reading in the content subjects, and
for the development of strong motives for independent reading
during free periods. But it is not sufficient merely to stimulate
interest in reading; in addition, reading interests and tastes
must be graded steadily upwards. Accordingly, superior
instruction aims to cultivate hearty enjoyment of good literature
and to elevate reading tastes. The values of these aims is
obvious. On the other hand, the need of directing increased
attention to them in both elementary and secondary schools is
very urgent. This fact is emphasized by the character of much of
the free reading of children and young people today. Numerous
studies show clearly that a surprisingly large percent of the
books and magazines read independently are of little value*

from either a social or a cultural point of view, if indeed they are not harmful or degrading. Furthermore, there is apparent lack of desirable standards in selecting material to read, also lack of appreciation of the better types of literature.

In partial explanation of this situation, several facts may be presented. First, the cultivation of hearty enjoyment of good literature which is often introduced very effectively in the kindergarten and primary grades thru [through] story telling and dramatization is discontinued in many schools during the middle grades. It is very unfortunate that little effort should be made to cultivate desirable standards and tastes during a period when children are beginning to read widely and when interests and tastes can be easily cultivated. Second, prevailing methods of teaching literature in the high school often fail to cultivate hearty enjoyment and to inspire pupils to continue the independent reading of superior types of literature. Third, many pupils in the grades and high school fail to receive adequate guidance and stimulation with respect to free reading....

The wisdom of providing specific guidance in cultivating appreciation of good literature is often questioned. The argument is advanced that appreciation cannot be taught; that it is acquired solely thru [through] wide reading of interesting, wholesome books and selections. Without depreciating in the least the importance of such reading, the position taken here is that specific guidance and leadership are highly desirable. This view is supported both by classroom experience and by the results of experiments....

The primary aim of the literature period is to cultivate hearty enjoyment in reading worthwhile books and selections. As pointed out by the National Committee on Reading, good literature is "most appreciated and makes its best contribution when it is approached in a recreational mood of curiosity" and not as study or work. One of the first requisites is that the child's early contacts with literature should be very interesting and pleasurable. To this end the kindergarten teacher reads and tells many interesting stories to young children and provides them with attractive picture books. During the primary grades, teachers provide many pleasurable contacts with good literature through dramatizations, the story hour, the language period, and frequent recreational reading periods. In this connection, the importance of reading for sheer fun and pleasure cannot be overemphasized. During the middle grades well-planned group activities, related to interesting themes, should be supplemented by much independent reading of good literature in which interest has been aroused during class periods. Furthermore, there must be much group reading for fun, frequent occasions to hear selections of good literature, particularly poems, read orally, and much sharing of experiences. During the high school period many units should be taught primarily to contribute genuine pleasure, to awaken new interests, and to cultivate favorable attitudes toward the better types of literature.

A second aim of the literature period is to broaden desirable reading interests. Striking evidence of the need of this step is found in the fact that children read only one or more types of material, such as series books. To overcome this difficulty, they should be introduced at frequent intervals to new fields of interest and to literary types which they might not discover without guidance. Records of actual experience should not be neglected, however. These include selections related to personal matters such as home or school life, to people and events in different times and places, to different phases of man's activity, to various human relationships such as good fellowship and loyalty to country, to current events, to contemporary social problems, as well as to life as presented in the great masterpieces of literature. It is true that many of the types of material mentioned belong properly in the content subjects. It is necessary to include some of them also in the literature period for the specific purpose of extending the range of hearty enjoyment and desirable reading interests.

The literature period has unique opportunities to extend and enrich the experiences of pupils far beyond the limits of other school subjects and activities and to aid in cultivating socially desirable attitudes, standards, and ideals. The National Committee on Reading rightly emphasized the fact that by *"acquainting pupils with the greatest and finest sources of genuine experience during the hours of recreation and true enjoyment in school, we may surely and wholesomely stimulate their interest in their life to be lived in books and broaden their interest to include new and excellent types of experience everywhere." By acquainting them with records of high achievement and noble character, desirable attitudes, standards, and ideals may be developed.*

Additional aims which merit strong emphasis during the literature period are to acquaint pupils with the sources and values of different types of literature including the better types of current literature, to cultivate appropriate habits of interpretative and critical thinking in various fields of literature, and to cultivate increasing preference for artistic forms of literature. These and other worthy aims offer a mighty challenge to teachers of reading and literature in elementary and secondary schools. The opportunity and the responsibility should not be neglected. (Gray, 1931, pp. 89–90)

Grouping for Reading

Grouping children for reading has been the subject of continued debate and discussion among reading educators for many years. Various plans have been developed, ranging from the traditional three groups of high-, middle-, and low-ability students to a more homogeneous arrangement. Specific criteria for grouping have varied widely as well. In the following discussion, Gray (1925) suggests specific criteria for grouping, as well as a plan for actual implementation of his ideas. Note his emphasis on the importance of measurement of capacity or intelligence. Consider Gray's recommendations and whether you agree or disagree.

At least three types of information are desirable at the beginning of the first grade in classifying pupils [for instruction in reading]. The first relates to their capacity to learn. For this purpose many schools give [a variety of either individual or group intelligence tests]. [Second] The results of one of more such tests should be supplemented by information concerning a child's home, his parents, his nationality, the condition of his health, physical defects, emotional and volitional traits, and his social adaptability. A third type of information relates to the extent and scope of his previous training, the general range of his experience, the facility with which he uses ideas, the extent of his vocabulary, his use of oral English, the accuracy of his enunciation and pronunciation, his attitude toward pictures, stories, and books, and his desire to learn to read.

Various plans have been followed in securing the information that is needed:

(a) In some schools it is collected during the kindergarten period, recorded on individual cards and passed on to the first grade with comments and suggestions by the teachers. This plan makes possible the classification of pupils in the first grade as soon as group intelligence tests have been given.

(b) In other schools individual or group mental tests are given in the kindergarten, and the pupils are classified on the basis of these scores when admitted to the first grade. Changes in their classification are made later if teachers secure evidence to justify them. The children who have not had kindergarten training are given group intelligence tests on entering school and are assigned to classes on the basis of the test scores until more detailed information can be secured.

(c) In still other schools all pupils are given group intelligence tests on entering first grade and are temporarily assigned to classes on the basis of the mental-test scores. A week or more is then devoted to oral exercises and interesting group activities in order to secure information concerning the accomplishments, needs, and characteristics of each pupil. The information secured in this way is recorded on individual cards and passed on to the teachers to whom the pupils are finally assigned. (pp. 32–33)

REFERENCES

Dewey, J. (1900). *School and society*. Chicago: University of Chicago Press.

Gates, A.I. (1960/1961, March). William Scott Gray, 1885–1960: Results of teaching a system of phonics. *The Reading Teacher, 14*, 248–252.

Gray, W.S. (1925). Reading activities in school and society. In G.M. Whipple (Ed.), *The twenty-fourth yearbook of the National Society for the Study of Education, Part I* (pp. 1–18). Bloomington, IL: Public School Publishing.

Gray, W.S. (1931). Enjoyment of good literature. *The Journal of the National Education Association, 20*, 89–90.

Gray, W.S. (1954). Nature of mature reading. In H.M. Robinson (Ed.), *Promoting maximal reading growth among able learners* (pp. 11–15). Chicago: University of Chicago Press.

Gray, W.S. (1958). Objectives for the new reading program. In H.M. Robinson (Ed.), *Evaluation of reading* (pp. 9–14). Chicago: University of Chicago Press.

Reflections

The following questions are designed to encourage you to reflect on Gray's work, especially in relation to the role of the classroom teacher of reading.

1. Gray identified four major goals for an effective classroom reading program, and he believed strongly in the importance of the teacher's role in implementing these ideas. Identify specific ways in which you might incorporate these ideas in your own teaching.

2. Although Gray's remarks on the extended use of good literature are over 70 years old, they are still relevant to today's classroom reading program. Offer some reasons to explain why teachers do not use good literature in their teaching, and how you might change this in your own classroom reading program?

FURTHER READING

Guthrie, J.A. (Ed.). (1985). *Reading: A research retrospective*. Newark, DE: International Reading Association.
> This monograph discusses the extensive and varied literacy research of Gray, noting the impact of his work on both the fundamental study of the reading process, as well as classroom applications.

Mavrogenes, N.A. (1985). *William S. Gray and the Dick and Jane readers*. (ERIC Document Reproduction Service No. ED 269 722)
> This publication provides an interesting discussion of Gray's influence on the development and writing of one of the most influential basal reading series in the United States.

Stevenson, J.A. (1985). *William S. Gray: Teacher, scholar, leader*. Newark, DE: International Reading Association.
> This volume provides an excellent overview of Gray's personal life, as well as his work as a literacy teacher and scholar. Of particular importance are the more than 500 bibliographic listings of his work.

Reading was the most important subject in our early American schools and it has continued to be the most important subject all through the years of our national growth.

I would hope that somehow we could instill within all parents the concept that the way in which they could make the greatest contribution to reading improvement is to give their whole-hearted loyalty and support to the public schools and to the personnel now dealing with their children.

Phonics is just one part of the total word-recognition program. Teachers not only teach phonics...but they equip the child with several other word-getting techniques, as well.

We need to develop discriminating readers: readers who will choose to read those things which will contribute most to their lives culturally, socially, and informatively.

Nila Banton Smith (1889–1976)

Although Nila Banton Smith is most noted for her work in the history of reading instruction, her body of research and writing encompasses most every aspect of reading instruction. Smith's professional career included work as a classroom teacher, university professor, and school administrator. Her dissertation, completed at Columbia University in 1934, was the basis for the book *American Reading Instruction* (see Further Reading, p. 45), considered a classic in the field of reading history. Although others have added to the original work in the intervening years, this volume is used often as a starting point in historical studies in reading education.

Nila Banton Smith's writings focused mostly on the classroom setting and the role of the effective teacher of reading. Topics such as the role of phonics, the use of various types of reading materials, and appropriate assessment methods in reading were frequently addressed in her professional work. Smith's textbook *Reading Instruction for Today's Children* (1963) was widely used in training classroom teachers in the field of reading education.

Throughout her professional career, Smith returned frequently to the theme of the importance of an historical perspective in the field of reading education. She believed that to evaluate a new development properly, it was necessary to consider what had been done in the past. Often this historical perspective identified "new and innovative practices" as nothing more than a repetition of past reading methods.

Nila Banton Smith was described as a person who never lost touch with the classroom, the student, or the teacher, and these recurring themes dominated her professional work.

Excerpts From the Writing of Nila Banton Smith

In the following discussion, Smith (1955a) presents a national challenge for reading. Although written in 1955, many of the "musts" she mentions are as relevant today as they were then. Note especially her comments about developing in students wide interests in reading, as well as critical reading.

Reading "Musts"

We are on the brink of a new epoch in reading instruction. Our "musts" are clearly defined. We have but to observe the onrush of social forces about us, to feel the impact of the new psychologies and philosophies, to examine the recent researches of educational investigators in order to know that reading instruction must change in many ways.

In the future, reading instruction must concern itself with much more than pedagogy. It must mesh more directly into the gears of pressing social problems and needs. It must make its contribution to American living and American ideals....

But now the situation has changed. Again we find America thrust into a period of insecurity. The strong young nation which our forefathers founded so well is challenged in its survival. Is it not time for us to take stock of our urgent social problems and to examine the contribution which reading instruction might make to the exigencies of American life? If the answer is "Yes," then the "musts" below are in order.

Develop Carry-Over Interests

We must strive, as we have never striven before, to develop wide, permanent, carry-over interests in reading. Social change is striding across the reading habits of America with a heavy tread. Reading is now faced with many competing agencies. Radio, television, movies, and picture magazines afford the average person about all the entertainment and information that he desires. Rather than accept a brief summary of news items from a commentator, together with his particular interpretation, citizens of America need to read widely for themselves, to sift, personally, the wheat from the chaff and to draw their own conclusions. All this means that we must exert ourselves as never before in developing vigorous, permanent interests in reading.

To develop more abiding interests, instruction in reading must be made increasingly attractive to children. Teachers must put to work all their enthusiasm, energy, wisdom, and ingenuity, not only in making the most of every reading situation which arises, but also in causing every reading activity to be a fascinating one to pursue.

More challenging materials are needed. Children of today are sophisticated; much of the material they are supposed to read in school is below their level of intelligence and understanding. Perhaps one reason why they enjoy television and movies so much is that these conveyors of entertainment and information do not talk down to them, and because they deal with subjects wider in scope and more mature in content than those dealt with in many school texts. Children must be surrounded with quantities of books dealing with an almost endless variety of subjects. The present day child is far beyond the naive simplicity which characterized the child of a generation ago. We must meet him on his own ground and in his own world if we expect to deepen and hold his interest in reading.

Stimulate Thoughtful Reading

Not only must we develop a more gripping interest in reading, but we must also develop the ability and habit of abstracting deeper meanings from what we read. If future America is to meet its pressing problems, it must be an informed America. An informed American must understand fully what it is that he is reading. Passive acceptance of surface meanings is not enough. We need to think as we read. All too often experiences which children receive in working with meanings in the classroom are those in which not much thinking is done. It is the type in which they simply give back some statement from the text. "What was Mary playing with?" and the text says, "Mary was playing with her doll."

The teacher of today must stimulate children to react in many different ways to the meanings which reading conveys. Children must be taught to question, reason, compare, draw inferences, generalize, interject ideas of their own, seek interaction of these ideas with others, and to draw independent conclusions. Thinking in connection with reading must be cultivated vigorously in order that deeper meanings behind the *symbols and between the lines may be sensed, and so that the real significance of statements may be completely understood.*

Emphasize Critical Analysis

Important as this matter of grasping deeper meanings is, we must not stop even at this point. We must go still further. In this age of high-pressure salesmanship and wide dispersal of propaganda we must place much more emphasis upon critical reading. Critical reading calls for additional steps in thinking. It involves getting the facts and interpreting deeper meanings, as discussed above. It also makes use of the personal judgment of the reader in deciding upon the validity of content. In critical reading, the reader evaluates and passes judgment upon the purpose, the fair-mindedness, the bias, the truthfulness of statements made in text. Teaching youth to detect slants and technics of the propagandist; teaching them to judge the validity of statements in printed materials they read are definite "musts." (Smith, 1955a, pp. 7–10)

The Phonics Controversy

One of the most controversial topics in reading education today is the teaching of phonics. Although it may seem that this debate is of recent origin, Smith identifies in her writing three or more past periods of history in which the teaching of phonics dominated reading education. In the following selection, Smith (1962) traces the history of the use of phonics in U.S. education. Although she compares phonics specifically to what she calls the "word method," any number of other reading philosophies or methods could be substituted in its place.

> *The critical attacks on reading instruction in the United States seem to spring from two basic assumptions: (1) that the children of America are not reading as well now as in former times, and (2) that the reason for the lowered achievement is the exclusive use of the word method, which some have dubbed "the cancer of configuration." The critics are arbitrarily campaigning for the return of phonics to the schools as the only way in which literacy in future America can be ensured.*

Phonics vs. Word Method

First, I should like to discuss the phonics versus word method controversy. Both phonics and word method have had peripatetic existences in American history. First one is in and the other is out, and vice versa. This is an old, old story.

For the first 175 years of our history, children learned to read without benefit either of word method or phonics. Then after the Revolution phonics entered the scene. Noah Webster was concerned about unifying the various languages spoken in America. He analyzed the English language into sound elements, prepared his Blue-Back Speller based on these elements, and launched it in the schools. He assumed that if all children learned to sound the letters, all of them would pronounce words in the same way.

Webster's phonic method was used for several years, then around 1840 certain American educators came back from visits to Prussia, telling how instructors were initiating children into reading by teaching them whole words. Soon after, readers based on the word method appeared, and this method was widely used until about 1890. This is the only period in American history in which educators and authors of readers have advocated the word method as a basic method of teaching reading.

About 1890 complaints arose similar to the ones that we hear now. Children weren't reading well, and it was all blamed on the word method. A sharp reversal of practice followed. Elaborate phonic systems were evolved and new readers were published in which children were started out in first grade memorizing letter sounds, and most of the reading time in the first grade was devoted to drill on phonic elements. This appears to be the sort of thing that certain critics want us to return to.

The extreme emphasis on phonics in beginning reading and throughout first grade characterized the most widely-used method until about 1920. Then we departed from phonics again. The scientific movement in education emerged between 1910 and 1920. Standardized reading tests appeared for the first *time. As a result of administering these tests in school systems, school people were appalled to discover the extremely large number of children who were not reading well, or often not at all. Many of the pupils who were reading were simply calling words and didn't know what they were reading about. Now extreme emphasis on phonics was blamed. Silent reading with emphasis on meaning came in, and phonics was practically abandoned for about 15 years. If this were the period in which the critics say we were not teaching phonics, they would be right. But this period has long since been dimmed in the annals of history.*

About 1935 schools again became deeply concerned about the numbers of children who were not learning to read. They re-examined phonics, and some investigators carried on studies revealing that phonics was effective. The method began to come back gradually, and it has been coming back ever since. During the last 10 years phonics has been taught more generally and more extensively than at any time since the early 1900s. Basic reader systems of today provide a phonics program embracing all important phonic elements contained in Webster's original analysis of the English language, and all reading series advocate the teaching of phonics from first grade through sixth, as well as stressing other word attack skills. Dr. Allen Barton [1961] reported, as a part of the Columbia-Carnegie study, that teachers throughout the country believed overwhelmingly in the teaching of phonics, and they believed also that other methods of word attack needed to be taught. Dr. Mary Austin [1962], in her preliminary report of the Harvard-Carnegie study, stated that she found no school system which omitted phonics, and that all except one mixed phonics with other word attack skills.

One of the chief differences between the phonics of the early 1900s and the present phonics is that the phonics of yesteryear was taught in one large dose in beginning first grade, while the present practice is to start children out reading experience stories, and they are taught auditory and visual discrimination informally as a foundation for phonics. As soon as initial interest in reading, attitude toward reading for meanings, and foundations of desirable eye movements are established, then phonics proper is taught in the first grade and throughout all of the other elementary grades. Phonics, however, is not generally used exclusively as a method of attack. The word recognition program in the elementary grades is strengthened by teaching the use of context clues, structural analysis and dictionary skills, as well as phonics.

So in response to the criticisms dealing with phonics versus word method we can say:

1. *The exclusive use of word method probably does not exist in any school in the country today.*

2. *The type of phonic teaching which the critics are urging was abandoned in our schools some 40 years ago because such large numbers of children were not learning to read.*

3. *Phonics is taught today, not only in first grade but in all six of the elementary grades. (Smith, 1962, pp. 146–148)*

Smith (1955b) continues to discuss phonics and the controversy surrounding it. Note the parallels in the role of phonics in reading education during the period in which she wrote and now. In particular, note the characteristics of phonics instruction that she identifies as reflecting a more current view.

Phonics has had a long history in America. During its history, phonics has undergone many changes. There have been changes in the time at which phonics has been introduced, changes in the organization of phonic content, and changes in the methods of teaching phonics.

The fact that instruction in phonics has endured through all these years attests to its value. The fact that it has undergone so many changes attests to the open-mindedness of school people, their willingness to modify practices, and their continuous quest for improvement.... (p. 73)

Recent professional books on reading offer evidence that phonics is recognized and recommended at the present time. An examination of the teachers' manuals which accompany eight leading series of basic readers currently used in our schools reveals that all of these series, without exception, provide a definite program in phonics as one of several word-recognition techniques. And this more direct instruction extends throughout the elementary grades in a carefully planned program of instruction.

Courses of study recently developed by public school systems most certainly testify to the fact that phonics is taught at the present time. Several courses of study in reading, published between 1948 and 1955, were selected at random as representing school systems in different parts of the country. Every course examined recommended work in phonics throughout all of the elementary grades.

Thus it is that one finds abundant evidence on all sides that American schools are teaching phonics at the present time. Professional books on reading, manuals of basic reading series, and courses of study in reading, all offer silent testimony to this fact.

Some of the characteristics which distinguish present-day instruction in phonics from that of the past are as follows:

- *Instruction in phonics is no longer used as an approach to beginning reading, nor is the word method used as an approach. The approach today is eclectic.*

- *While instruction in phonics, per se, is postponed beyond beginning stages, the foundation for it is laid from the very beginning through the use of rhyming and matching activities designed to develop auditory and visual discrimination.*

- *Phonics is no longer confined to the first grade as was the case in years gone by. It is taught throughout the elementary grades. Schools now have a much more extensive program than formerly.*

- *Teachers no longer use organized lists of "family words" as the chief content of instruction in phonics. They prefer*

*to teach phonic elements as children need them in
learning new words in their immediate reading.*

- *Phonics is just one part of the total word-recognition
program. Teachers do not only teach phonics more
extensively than ever before but they equip the child with
several other word-recognition techniques as well. (Smith,
1955b, pp. 75–76)*

A frequent criticism of reading instruction is that there seems to be
more cases of reading disability today than there were in the past. In the
following passage, Smith (1962) discusses this so-called current "problem," using a medical example.

*Critics also question the number of remedial cases in the
schools of today. Usually they add something like this: "We
never heard about remedial cases when I was in school," and
this is supposed to be a sort of barb because we have so many
remedial cases at present.*

*Let me answer this question with an example from the field
of medicine. I was in the home of a physician a few evenings
ago and I repeated to him a question which I recently had heard
an elderly gentleman ask. The question was, "Is this heart attack
malady something new? I never heard about it when I was a
boy."*

*"Of course he didn't hear about heart attacks because
doctors didn't recognize the symptoms of heart attacks at that
time," was the reply. "They diagnosed and treated other kinds of
heart trouble but not the heart attacks you hear about today."*

*Then my physician friend went on to explain that for many
years this affliction was treated as acute indigestion. When
individuals had what is now commonly known as a heart attack
they were given medicine for stomach trouble, and hundreds
were dying with what was mistakenly called "acute indigestion."
It was not until the early 1900s that Dr. James Herrick of Rush
Medical College wrote his classic work on coronary thrombosis,
a clot in a coronary artery. Dr. Herrick delineated the affliction
and its symptoms so clearly that the average clinician was then*

able to identify it, understand it, and treat it. Now we never hear of "acute indigestion," but we frequently hear of "heart attacks."

I'm sure you sensed my intended analogy long before the heart attack story was finished. Just let me say briefly that the science of remedial reading also has developed tremendously in recent years. We now know how to identify remedial readers, because we have developed ways of diagnosing and treating them. And along with these developments the term "remedial readers" has become as common as "heart attacks." The layman often jumps to the conclusion that since he has only heard about remedial readers in fairly recent years that we didn't have them in the good (?) old days.

Furthermore: not all remedial cases are word recognition cases. It follows, therefore, that inability to use phonics is not necessarily the sine qua non *at the root of all reading disability. As we all know, reading deficiency may be due to lack of intelligence, brain damage, neurological defects, physical diseases, language handicaps, lack of experiential background, emotional disturbances, and so on. How naive the critics are in claiming that all reading disability is due to the fact that we don't start children out sounding letters immediately upon entrance into the first grade! (pp. 148–149)*

New Concepts of Reading Evaluation

In the following selection, Smith (1960) describes the primary reasons for the use of both standardized and informal reading tests. Of particular interest, she suggests how classroom teachers can go beyond the more traditional forms of reading evaluation by using a series of self questions.

Just a word about evaluation of reading achievement which seems to be taking on new forms. For many years, we measured effects of reading instruction formally with standardized tests given at the beginning and end of each semester. We still are doing this and it is desirable to do so, providing the test results are interpreted in terms of the personal equipment, opportunities, and abilities of each individual child.

In addition to using standardized tests, teachers have evaluated each child informally each time he has read by answering herself such questions as "Is he able to successfully attack and pronounce more new words by himself?" "Is he growing in ability to answer questions on the content?" "Is he reading with greater fluency?" We are still noting these evidences of growth in the mechanics of reading, and it is important that we continue to do so. But new concepts of evaluation of reading growth are emerging—concepts which are broader and deeper than those only concerned with mechanics of reading. Many teachers are now evaluating the reading of a pupil not only in noting such items as I have mentioned but also with such concerns as these:

> Was this reading experience sufficiently satisfying to aid in developing in this child a sense of personal dignity and worth and achievement?
>
> Have new interests arisen which will lead on to further reading?
>
> Has worthwhile information been acquired from the reading content?
>
> Has the child done some real thinking in connection with the reading content?
>
> Have deeper insights into human living and deeper understandings of human relationships been developed from the import of the content reading or from the discussion concerning it?
>
> Is this child increasing his ability to evaluate his own growth in reading?

And, certainly in this searching for evidences of child growth, the teacher will include the question: "Is he extending and refining the reading skills that he will need in realizing his goals in school, in his life's work, in his recreational pursuits?"

And as for the teacher, herself, in applying the newer ideas, the teacher needs continuously to evaluate herself in new ways. She needs to search intensively for the answers to such questions as these:

> *Am I deepening my own insights in regard to the total growth of each child as well as his reading growth?*
>
> *Am I providing reading experiences which are simple and interesting enough to be satisfying but difficult enough in learning elements to enable each one to stretch toward higher realization of his abilities?*
>
> *Am I willing to permit each child to be his own age and to do what he is ready to do?*
>
> *Am I looking for weaknesses as well as strengths in children's learning to read?*
>
> *Am I seeking the causes of the weaknesses?*
>
> *Am I improving my own skills of evaluation?*
>
> *Am I frankly acknowledging the fact that some of the child's weaknesses may be due to my teaching?*
>
> *Am I examining both my strengths and weaknesses objectively, and facing my weaknesses with renewed efforts to improve?*

The teacher who evaluates herself continuously in regard to the deeper growths of human beings as well as growth in reading achievement will probably be successful in applying any of the new ideas which are in our midst at the present time or which are likely to develop in the future. She will dare to try new ideas, she will know how to judge their worth, she will be able to adjust them in ways most conducive to growth in the particular children with whom she is working. (Smith, 1960, pp. 373–374)

REFERENCES

Austin, M. (1962). *Harvard-Carnegie Study. A preliminary report.* Presented at the Seventh Annual Convention of the International Reading Association, San Francisco.

Barton, A. (1961, September). Report given at A Policy Conference on Reading, James Conant (Chair), New York.

Smith, N.B. (1955a). Reading "musts" contribute to living. *Reading for Today's Children: Thirty-fourth Yearbook of the National Elementary Principal.* Washington, DC: National Educational Association.

Smith, N.B. (1955b). Phonics in beginning reading: Review and evaluation. *The Reading Teacher, 9,* 73, 75–76.

Smith, N.B. (1960). Something old, something new in primary reading. *Elementary English, 37,* 373–374.

Smith, N.B. (1962). Some answers to criticisms of American reading instruction. *The Reading Teacher, 16,* 146–150.

Smith, N.B. (1963). *Reading instruction for today's children.* New York: Prentice-Hall.

Reflections

Many of the current issues in reading education have been debated and discussed in the past and are illustrated in the historical research and writing of Nila Banton Smith. As you reflect on her writing consider the following:

1. Smith identifies "musts" for a classroom reading program. How are you implementing these ideas in your own reading program?

2. Smith addresses the question of phonics and effective reading instruction. Compare and contrast her ideas on this subject with your own.

FURTHER READING

Smith, N.B. (1934). *American reading instruction*. New York: Silver Burdett. (Reprinted in 1965 and 1986 by the International Reading Association, Newark, DE).
    This book is considered a classic in the field of the history of reading education and a foundational reference for the study of past developments in this field.

Smith, N.B. (1952). Historical turning points in reading. *National Education Association Journal, 41*, 280–282.
    In this article, through the use of a series of brief scenarios, Smith illustrates the most important developments in the history of reading instruction.

Smith, N.B. (1961). What have we accomplished in reading?—A review of the past fifty years. *Elementary English, 38*, 141–150.
    This article, written in honor of the 50th anniversary of the National Council of Teachers of English, highlights what Smith considered as the most important developments in the field of reading during a 50-year period.

It is impossible to set up, once and for all, a stipulated list of particular requirements for successful work in beginning reading in general. Reading is begun by very different materials, methods, and general procedures....

There is no such thing as an ideal or minimum mental age for learning to read. A child may be fully "ready" to learn under teacher A, but unequal to the more severe demands or the less skilled teaching of teacher B. We should, therefore, establish a policy of starting each child learning to read when he is sufficiently ready for the particular program and teacher he is to work with.

Teaching the alphabet before reading, conducting extensive phonetic and other drills upon isolated words before reading, and conducting the reading lessons mainly by asking children to read orally, in turn, are examples of formal, exacting and misleading practices which have been discarded as the result of careful investigation.

In wholehearted reading activity, the child does more than understand and contemplate: his emotions are stirred; his attitudes and purposes are modified; indeed, his inner most being is involved.

Arthur I. Gates (1890–1972)

*A*rthur Gates was a leading reading teacher and writer for more than 40 years. He is most noted for his research and study related to the psychology of reading, as well as the analysis and correction of reading difficulties. During his tenure at the Teachers College, Columbia University (New York), he wrote more than 300 books and articles. Some of his most noted works include the *Psychology of Disability in Reading and Spelling*, *The Improvement of Reading*, and *New Methods in Primary Reading*. He also developed a series of reading assessment procedures that were widely used in public schools for many years. These included general reading survey tests, as well as various types of diagnostic assessment instruments.

Gates's writing most notably involves a number of controversial reading issues that were of great concern to educators in the first half of the 20th century. For instance, a number of research studies published indicate that there was a minimal mental age that readers must attain before they could be expected to read. Although Gates agreed that mental ability was a critical aspect of reading growth, he objected to the idea that a specific point or score must be reached in order to achieve reading success. He also was concerned about a prevailing idea of the amount of time needed by a child to obtain certain predetermined physical, social, and mental abilities before the classroom teacher could effectively begin reading instruction. Gates clearly noted in his writing and speaking that, although the reading process was one that had many commonalties, each individual reader brought unique abilities and development traits to the learning process. Gates believed that no established set of prerequisites for reading success would ever apply fully to all readers.

The work of Arthur Gates still has important implications for today's reading teachers. For instance, his beliefs about reasons for the teaching of reading, his views of the roles of the reading teacher, and his thoughts about easy answers to reading instruction are as current as if they had been written yesterday. Gates saw the reading process as one unique to the individual reader and most importantly, that it was the effective classroom teacher who needed to build on this knowledge of each student's abilities.

Excerpts From the Writing of Arthur Gates

What Should Be Taught in Reading?

The following short essay is one of the best summaries of what reading teachers should be doing in their daily instruction. Note especially what Gates (1951) says about the relationship between the mechanics of reading and the more important goals of literacy instruction.

During the past 30 years we have learned many important facts about the ways children learn to read, about the methods which are successful in teaching them to read, and about the skills which they need to establish sound reading habits. We have learned so much about the technicalities of learning to read that is seems we now face a real danger—the old one—of not being able to see the forest for the trees. For in our intense concentration, the mechanics of reading—on word analysis and word recognition skills, on phonics, on eye training and coordination, etc.—we have perhaps lost sight of the real goals of the teaching of reading.

There can be but two real goals toward which we aim in teaching reading—or, more precisely, a single goal with two aspects: to teach children to read well and to love to read. For unless they learn to read well, children will not love to read; and unless they love to read they will not read well.

The reading teacher should never become so engrossed with mechanics or so intent on skill that she loses sight of this dual objective. Every day she should ask herself, "Are my pupils reading soundly and, most important, do they really love it?"

What Is Involved?

What is involved in reading well deserves a few words of explanation. First, to be able to read well the child must, from the beginning, read naturally and freely. He must have ample experience in reading as freely and naturally as an adult does when he relaxes after dinner and takes up his favorite book or newspaper or magazine. Many children have spent three or more years in school without ever having read this way. What they have been doing is laboriously translating printed words just as an adult does when he begins to read a foreign language in a series of hard lessons. A child may be average or superior in phonetic analysis or even able to "work out" more printed words than the average pupil in his class, and still be unable to really read well. Unless the conditions are provided which enable a child to really read freely and naturally from the earliest stages, he is unlikely to read well or to love to read.

Reading well is something very different from being able merely to recognize printed phonograms and words or even to pronounce the series of words in a sentence. The child who is adept at doing auditory gymnastics with phonetic elements may be a poor reader. Learning to recognize an unusually large number of words "by sight" in the first grade is likely to develop a distorted skill which is not reading and which, indeed, may even interfere with learning to read well. The pupil who develops extraordinary skill in guessing words from context may have so neglected the ability to use the helpful usual and auditory clues in word forms as to become a word guesser instead of a well-rounded reader.

Need Array of Techniques

No, learning to recognize words or to employ a series of word-analysis and other techniques is not learning to read well. Good, natural reading requires a properly balanced and unified array of techniques. It needs a highly co-coordinated unity of skills. No mere series or collection or sum of the particular techniques enables a child to read well. The test of success in teaching reading is not how well the pupil can perform in any of the component skills (such as sounding letters or phonograms, recognizing words, or moving the eyes along the line) but how well he really reads and how much he enjoys doing it.

This is not to say that techniques are unimportant. The contrary is true. Techniques must be taught. They must be the best ones. They must be neither overtaught nor undertaught and they must work together in such coordination to produce the smooth total activity which good reading is. To do this requires careful, shrewd guidance.

In learning any complex skill, there is the temptation to adopt the method which produces a quick display of results. For example, a person turned loose with a typewriter without expert guidance is likely to use only a few fingers in a hunt-and-hit procedure. This enables him to get obvious results quickly. He can hit off a paragraph right away. But he is not typing well nor is he learning to type well. If he persists, he will not only have to learn the whole sound process later, but also unlearn a lot of interfering techniques. And one sees very few hunt-and-hit typists who love to type.

Teachers of reading are faced with this temptation. The social pressure to make a quick showing of some kind of skill in reading is very great. And there are numerous schemes offered to the teacher every year which are guaranteed to produce these quick results—usually some sort of highly formalized phonetic drill. But the final result of this kind of teaching is doomed to be the same as with hunt-and-hit typing. The flashy starter sooner or later falls behind those with sound techniques, and he either quits the activity or is relegated to the lowest group. The child with unsound reading techniques, however spectacular his beginning, eventually finds himself an inefficient and bored reader struggling along until remedial reading is provided.

The importance of developing the harmonious whole process involved in sound reading, and avoiding the distortions of overdeveloped isolated skills and techniques, however spectacular the stunts they make possible, can hardly be overestimated. Progress must be sound and sure even if it is slower and superficially less showy.

What Is Essential?

Children must acquire sound techniques to read well, and ability to read well is essential to learning to love to read. But, to read well and to love it requires that the reading program provide an abundance of opportunity to read naturally and successfully. Every person has his limits within which he can read well. A typical sound third-grade reader can read well and enjoy reading material of modest difficulty, but a Shakespeare play is too difficult for him. Force him to do all or most of his reading beyond the level at which he can read soundly with understanding and enjoyment, and you will soon destroy both interest and ability. You will also destroy the child's confidence and his sense of security. Both are essential to effective learning.

The regular basal reading program should provide the child with a wealth of enjoyable material on his own reading level. Over and above this, there should be available to him a library table or corner which abounds in interesting and lively stories and informational reading material on the level at which he is able to read well, and the day's schedule should provide time for him to enjoy these materials—to read freely and naturally with the same freedom from difficulty and the same smoothness which characterize an adult's personal reading.

This free reading, without stops to struggle with difficulties with unfamiliar words and constructions, is just as important, indeed it is probably more important, for the poor reader than for the superior reader. The poorer reader is precisely the one who is most readily bored by formal drill materials and who most seriously needs the assurance and satisfaction that can come only from reading really interesting stories.

We must give added emphasis to this matter of interesting children in reading. All the skills, all the techniques, all the mechanics, are only tools to use in learning to read well so as to be able to enjoy reading. We must not lose sight of the fact that they are only tools—useful, important, necessary tools, but still tools—means to the end but not the end itself. We must not so emphasize them that our pupils cease to enjoy reading. We must give children interesting material of suitable difficulty, provide them with simple but sound guidance, and give them ample opportunity to read by themselves and to learn to read better in the course of reading. Given these basal things, they will learn to read soundly and to love it, and we will then have achieved the real goal of teaching reading. (Gates, 1951, pp. 13–14)

Mental Age and Reading

The precise relation between a reader's mental age or intelligence level and reading ability has been one of longstanding interest to classroom teachers. This interest was most evident in determining whether there was a minimum level of mental development and an optimum age to begin formal reading instruction. One of the most famous (or infamous, depending on your viewpoint) reading studies was done by Morphett and Washburn (1931). They suggested that regular reading instruction not begin until a student reached the mental age of 6 years, 6 months. Gates (1937) and other writers at that time were quick to question this conclusion and, in the following passage, give reasons for this decision. For the modern teacher it is important to note that even today there are no absolute guidelines that will clearly determine when a student is ready to begin reading.

> For some time the problem of determining the optimum or necessary mental age level at which reading can be successfully introduced has been under investigation. Recently, in books written primarily for professional workers, statements have been made which implied that this problem is fairly well solved. Such statements usually imply, more specifically, that success with typical first-grade reading programs requires a stipulated mental age, six and a half years being the age usually given.
>
> The fact remains, however, that it has been by no means proved as yet that a mental age of six and one half years is a proper minimum to prescribe for learning to read by all types of teaching skill and procedures. Representative data gathered by the writer indicate rather clearly that statements concerning the necessary mental age at which a pupil can be entrusted to learn to read are essentially meaningless. The age for learning to read under one program or teaching method may be entirely different from that required under other circumstances. The crucial mental age will vary with the materials; the type of instruction; the skill of the teacher; the size of the class; the amount of preceding preparatory work; the frequency and the treatment of special difficulties, such as visual defects; and other factors. (p. 42)

Technology and Reading

Today, technology has influenced all aspects of our lives and is certainly true in the area of reading instruction. For instance, in recent years, there have been many new literacy materials related to the personal computer and the use of the Internet. In the following passage, Gates (1967) addresses these developments with a word of caution to classroom teachers. Note his concern about an anticipated flood of new reading products, often developed by those with little or no experience in reading instruction. As you read, substitute the word *computer* for *programmed materials*.

> At this point, however, a word of caution is in order concerning the use of new technology. The next few years will witness a flood of new programmed materials, teaching machines, canned television and sound-motion picture sequences, "skill-builder" booklets, phonic systems, workbooks, and other materials and gadgets. Many of these may be inexpertly conceived and hastily prepared. Sales campaigns of unprecedented vigor and volume may be launched. The panicky spirit of the times may feed the urge toward hasty changes. Under these circumstances, the classroom teacher should be calm and cautious. He should realize that a novice, untrained in the field of reading, is as unlikely to make a good program in reading as a hack songster is to compose a fine opera. Indeed, for precisely the reason that programmed material requires that the best general pattern of reading abilities be reduced to very minute and rigorously controlled steps, the highest degree of expertness is necessary. Teachers, however, should not be overawed by mechanical or psychological mysteries. Programmed materials are, after all, merely materials similar in nature to printed workbooks. Teachers should study and judge them with care and confidence.
>
> The heart of the teaching machine is the program which it presents. The teaching machine is merely a device, exactly as a sound motion picture projector is a mechanism for presenting material. The teaching machine program may be good or bad, exactly as a motion picture program may be. (pp. 25–27)

Gates (1967) described a type of early technology that was designed to help students increase their reading speed. It is included here, not so much because of its historical description of a speed reading machine, but rather because of his suggestions that perhaps the best way to help readers become better at reading is simply to read! In the last sentence, you might substitute "example of current reading technology" for the words, "device—mechanical or other" and use it to evaluate new reading instructional materials as they are developed.

This new type of teaching machine should not be confused, however, with certain other mechanical devices which have been developed as teaching aids. Each should be appraised in terms of certain principles. For example, machines which expose a line of print in parts, such as three or four phrases, one after another, are recommended to increase the rate of reading. While such a machine may have value for demonstration purposes, it does not really teach the pupil to read as he should read in a normal situation, and it forces him to learn adjustments that do not exist when he sits down to read a book by himself. A book will not conveniently flash the phrases one after another as the mechanical apparatus does. A pupil may learn to read "thought units" when the machine forces them on him, but he may read a book in quite another way. Another popular pacing machine requires that the teacher or pupil place a book under the metal covering, turn on the motor, and then try to keep reading the lines as a metal shutter moves down the page covering line after line. This calls for a less artificial departure from the natural situation than some other gadgets, but the same effect can be obtained with less distraction without the machine. All the pupil needs is a piece of cardboard which he himself moves down the page at a pace to suit his ability. He can force the pace as he desires; he can make it faster or slower or skip back and repeat a line as needed. Every such device—mechanical or other— should be appraised in terms of the extent to which it introduces artificial factors, distorts the natural process, or lacks proper flexibility and adaptability to the reader's needs. (pp. 25–27)

Teaching Reading Using Literature

Gates believed that, although the teaching of skills in a classroom reading program was important, teachers often overdid it to the determent of the reading of literature. In the following passage, Gates (1940) describes why he believed a literature based approach to reading was of greatest value in the teaching of reading.

Teaching methods as well as materials have an influence on reading interests and habits. The main fault in teaching today, I believe, is excess. It is necessary to have some sort of basal program of instruction to develop skills essential for efficient reading. Newer methods enable teachers to accomplish this purpose in less time and with richer concomitants than ever before. These methods require incentives for and checks upon speed, accuracy, fullness of understanding and validity of interpretation. Such analytic work is necessary but a small amount is sufficient. Only a fraction of the total time spent in reading should be devoted to this type of instruction, leaving several fold as much time for normal, undisturbed reading of literature.

A common mistake is to insist on the same or a similar type of teaching, employing supervision, recitation, comprehension exercises, discussion of issues, outlining, summarizing or whatnot in all or nearly all reading activities. This zeal to teach and test defeats its own purpose. Any normal adult would throw all his books and magazines out of the window and stalk off to the movies in a huff if he were repeatedly asked to spend his evenings reading his books and magazines for the purpose of answering certain questions asked in advance, or if after completing each article or chapter, he had to record his speed, take a series of comprehension exercises, write a summary or review, or tell what parts he liked best and why. Among my friends are a number of persons, including some authors of fiction, who read widely for the fun of it. When a visitor in a group of these people mentions a book and asks for responses, I have observed but one expression on their faces—an expression of deep anguish. Even in their lives, generous provision is made for wholly private reading for the jolly good fun of it. What they think about it before, during and after is nobody's business and to insist on inquisition is not only to violate one's privacy, it is also to interfere with one's recreational freedom. I have joined with several persons of my acquaintance in refusing to read, for purposes of review, any book I really want to read. It half spoils my enjoyment of a book to read with the realization that I must write or say something about it, even what I like or dislike, when I am through. This may be childish; in fact, I believe that is exactly what it is, and it bids me advise that children be left alone to read as they will without the cloud of irksome anticipation floating through their minds.

What has been said may lead some of you to inquire: "Well, is there any job at all for a teacher of reading and literature?" My answer is that there is less need for most of the simple, easy rule of thumb tasks, but very great need of a larger amount of much more difficult and subtle services, of which the following are the most important requirements:

1. *The teacher should know intimately the substance, difficulty, and other characteristics of hundreds of books and magazine articles for children and become familiar with new ones as they are published. Since every grade includes a wide range of reading ability, she must know the material for practically all grades from two to twelve. This task is a very exclusive one and it requires great sagacity as well as much time.*

2. *The teacher should know the reading interests and abilities of her pupils so well that she can give each wise guidance in locating the works that will be most interesting and educative for them. This assignment also requires much time spent in getting acquainted with all aspects of the life and activities of each pupil and it also requires very great psychological insight.*

3. *The teacher should be capable of arranging the conditions, giving the suggestions, and organizing the projects which will stimulate and sustain the pupil's*

desire to read. The traditional scheme of assigning readings, and trying to stir up interest by asking questions and talking about the selections in the class periods is a ridiculously naive oversimplification of the teaching process.

4. The teacher should be able to maneuver into operation various enterprises which give pupils opportunity to express themselves concerning their reading if they wish to do so, and to make fruitful use of what they have read. Here again, telling what they like or dislike, answering comprehension questions, explaining words, phrases or lines, writing reviews, etc., are quite unsatisfactory formal rules of thumb.

All these services must be achieved with such tact and skill that they never have the chilling effect of an assignment or order or interference or inquisition of pointless busy-work. To enrich and enliven literature for a boy or girl without disturbing the free spirit of a recreational enterprise is a difficult and subtle art. I feel frankly that if a teacher cannot do so, he had better do nothing at all except to suggest suitable books and leave the youngster alone with them. To do this well, I assure you, is a big achievement requiring extensive time and talent. To add to the understanding and enjoyment of literature as the musicians and actors in an opera increase the significance and appeal of the libretto—this should be the accepted objective of the teacher of literature and reading. That this requires effort and talent cannot be denied. Is there any real job for the teacher of literature? In my opinion, no assignment in the entire school curriculum calls for more intelligence and artistry than the teaching of reading and literature. (Gates, 1940, p. 162)

REFERENCES

Gates, A.I. (1937). The necessary mental age for beginning reading. *The Education Digest, 2*, 42–43.

Gates, A.I. (1940). Intelligence and artistry in teaching reading. *The Elementary English Review, 17*, 133–162.

Gates, A.I. (1951). What should we teach in reading? *School and Community, 37,* 13–14.

Gates, A.I. (1967). *What the research says to the teacher. Teaching reading* (pp. 25–27). Washington, DC: National Education Society, Department of Classroom Teachers.

Morphett, M.V., & Washburn, C. (1931). When should children learn to read? *The Elementary School Journal, 31,* 496–503.

Reflections

The following questions are designed to encourage you to consider Gates's work in relation to your own teaching of reading.

1. Based on Gates's comments and your own experiences as a reading teacher, what is the proper balance between learning specific reading skills and extended reading of literature?

2. What were Gates's primary concerns about purported "new" innovations in teaching reading, and how do they influence you in evaluating and using new reading methods and materials?

FURTHER READING

Gates, A.I. (1929). *The improvement of reading.* New York: Macmillan.
This textbook is an excellent reference on the teaching of reading. It contains excellent descriptions of classroom instruction in reading, particularly relating to text comprehension and remedial instruction.

Gates, A.I. (1931). New ways of teaching reading. *Parents Magazine, 6,* 18–19, 52–55.
This article written for parents reviews the then current thinking on the most effective ways of teaching reading. It is interesting to compare and contrast teaching reading in 1931 with today.

Gates, A.I. (1955). Why Mr. Flesch is wrong. *NEA Journal, 44,* 332–333.
This article presents Gates's response to the very controversial book by Rudolf Flesch (1955) titled *Why Johnny Can't Read,* which received wide publicity by the media. Despite the fact that this debate took place almost 50 years ago, many of the same issues are of concern in today's literacy community.

Reading is a language process rather than a school subject. In a psychological sense, reading is a thinking process. In another sense, reading is a social process that relates the reader to his environment.

[S]ystematic instruction for the development of efficient reading habits is the responsibility of every teacher.

Reading requires a "taking to" as well as a "taking from" a language situation. If reading abilities, skills, and attitudes are to be serviceable to the end that reading is to be promoted, then thought or meaning must be kept upper-most and the mechanics of the process must be reduced to automation.

Emmett Albert Betts (1903–1987)

*E*mmett Betts was an early leader in literacy education, with a professional career that lasted nearly 50 years. His educational experiences ranged over a wide spectrum that included classroom teacher, school administrator, and various university faculty positions. He is most widely known for his research and writing about various types of problem readers. His interest in children with severe reading problems led Betts to develop one of the first nationally recognized reading clinics in 1937. This facility at Pennsylvania State University (State College, Pennsylvania, USA), was designed with a twofold purpose: first, to help children and young adults who had severe reading disabilities; and second, to train education professionals in the diagnosis and effective treatment of language disorders.

Betts's writing was widely published (one source noted his total references exceeded 1,300). Of this material, his most noted works include *Prevention and Correction of Reading Difficulties* (1936), and *Foundations of Reading Instruction* (1946), which are considered by many reading authorities to be classic references in the field. He also compiled two important collections of reading research: (1) a bibliography (1934) on problems related to analysis, prevention, and correction of reading difficulties, containing references to 1,200 historical studies on diagnosis and remediation of reading difficulties; and (2) a bibliography (1945) that indexed professional literature on reading and related topics and included information on over 8,200 articles, books, and references in reading education from 1880 through 1945. Together these references constitute a thorough historical review of the field of reading education from its early inception to its development as an important educational discipline.

I included the work of Emmett Betts because of his pioneering acknowledgment that every reader is an individual with unique strengths and abilities in reading.

Excerpts From the Writing of Emmett Betts
Goals of an Effective Reading Program
Betts (1946) clearly stated his beliefs about the basic purposes of reading education. Note his emphasis on the importance of the effective reader as a productive member of society.

Purposes and objectives of reading instruction have been revised, broadened, and extended so that the modern school offers rich and worth-while reading experiences, the chief purpose of which is the preparation of the child for living in a democratic society. This is being achieved by differentiation in instruction and reduction of regimentation; by socialization of the objectives of reading instruction; by emphasis on meaning and critical interpretation rather than upon drill; by recognition of individual and group interests and needs; and by careful guidance in learning when to use language and when to listen as well as how to use language. Autocratic teaching is being superseded by techniques for educational guidance evolved in modern schools. Hence, the purpose of the modern school is the development of a wholesome personality based on social and emotional adjustment as contrasted to [only] the learning of subject-matter purposes of the traditional school.

In traditional schools, the objectives of reading instruction have been stated largely in terms of skills, abilities, and information to be learned. One of the chief differences between the objectives of traditional schools and those of modern schools is the emphasis on pupil attitudes. In modern schools, attitudes of approach receive major attention so that the child is motivated from within to acquire needed skills, abilities, and information. In short, incentives play a major role in traditional schools; motives in modern schools.

Reading came to be revered as a separate subject in the curriculum, in traditional schools. Reading instruction was administered on the assumption that reading had a subject matter of its own. When the children closed their books at the end of a reading lesson, instruction in reading ceased for the day. While this may have brought a sigh of relief, the pupils did not learn when to use reading as a learning aid in their other school and out-of-school activities and they did not learn how to read arithmetic, science, social science, and other instructional materials. As a result, reading was divorced from the problems of everyday living.

Using Reading as a Learning Aid

In modern schools, reading instruction is based on the notion that reading is a process, not a subject. Reading is conceived to be a social tool to meet social needs. The child lives in a language world where reading and listening play a dominant role in social and emotional adjustment. He is besieged on every side with billboards, books, newspapers, magazines, radio programs, and numerous other language barrages designed to influence his views and opinions. (Both dictators and democratic leaders are learning how to use language to influence people and make friends!) Since a reasonable degree of control over the reading process is vital to successful living in a democratic society, reading instruction is not limited to compartmentalized treatment in a separate period; instead, guidance is given in reading in all school activities so that it functions to the fullest extent in the child's out-of-school life. In this way, reading interests are broadened and attitudes of wanting to read are nourished. (Betts, 1946, pp. 83–84)

Differences in Reading Ability

Unfortunately, even today many reading programs seem to follow the general instructional philosophy that only one approach or reading technique fits all! In the following passage, Betts (1946) refutes this idea, noting many differences in the learning abilities and backgrounds of all children.

The wide range of capacities, abilities, needs, and interests in any classroom necessitates a differentiated approach to instruction in all school levels and in all areas of learning. Reading is a highly valued aid to learning. Children vary widely in their readiness to use this aid and in their control over this complex process.

Teaching is the practical recognition of differences. Until differences among the pupils of a given class are recognized, [reading instruction] cannot be on a sound, effective, systematic basis. A significant part of the dilemma in modern education has been brought about by a failure to admit differences—by the treating of all children alike.

A "class" or "grade" is an abstraction; it exists in the teacher's mind or nervous system. Actually, a class is comprised of Bobby, Johnny, Mary, Alice, etc.,—a group of individuals. These individuals vary widely in [reading] capacities, achievements, interests, etc. In a sound educational program, the practices must square with the facts. Regimented instruction (i.e., the use of the same materials for all the pupils of a "class" or "grade," etc.) must be justified on the basis of questionable assumptions, whereas the facts make differentiated instruction imperative. No one has ever seen a "first-grade class," or a "fifth-grade class." What a teacher should "see" is a group of individuals, unique unto themselves. Not until differences are "seen" is the teacher ready to teach, because learning the child must precede teaching him....

A program of differentiated [reading] instruction involves more than small group and individualized activities. It includes class planning and activities, group planning and activities, and individual planning and activities. Differentiated instruction is a way of evaluating and living with a group of individuals in a classroom that results in a maximum of development of each individual in terms of his interests, needs, and capacities. Through this type of classroom administration, basic reading skills, abilities, attitudes, and information are given life significance. (p. 3)

Reading as Only One Aspect of Language

As a language philosophy, the idea of reading as only one aspect of total communication has been ignored by many school literacy programs. Reading was taught as a separate subject, generally removed from writing, speaking, and listening. Today, the interrelatedness of all aspects of language is generally accepted among all reading teachers. In the following passage, Betts (1946) provides a rationale for this belief system, particularly as it relates to reading comprehension.

The sum total of language skills, abilities, attitudes, and information may be represented by a triangle, the area of the triangle representing language (see Figure). Since oral language is the child's first acquisition, the base of the triangle may be labeled speech. A second side of the triangle, is reading; the third side, writing, including spelling. Speech, reading, and writing are actually sides, or facets, of a large area of learning called language.

The diagram is not complete, however, when the triangle has been drawn, because language is symbolic. Meaning does not exist in words or combinations of words. Language must represent things—facts or experience—for the individual who is listening, speaking, reading, or writing. The speaker or the writer is expressing mental constructs; the listener or reader must reconstruct the facts behind the symbols. Meaning exists in the relationships between language and facts; that is, in the language-fact relationships. To isolate language from experience is to divorce it from reality. Hence, it is necessary to complete the diagram by adding a third dimension labeled experience. The diagram, therefore, will take the form of a three-sided solid, or prism. (Betts, 1946, pp. 9–10)

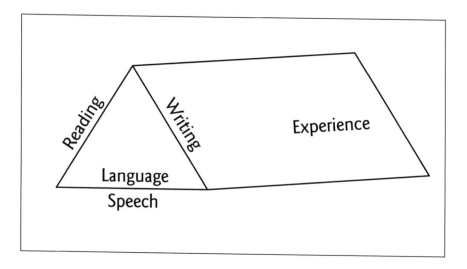

Reading Assessment and Teacher Evaluation

Today there is a frenzy of standardized testing. Although this is true across the curriculum, it is especially evident in reading education. Betts (1946) anticipated many of these current problems associated with reading and testing. In fact, the following selection seems as contemporary as if it had been taken from today's newspaper.

The use of standardized tests in some school situations can be questioned. First, in some schools there appears to be a tendency to emphasize the average class achievement and to disregard the wide range of differences that exist in a given class or grade. This inadequate interpretation of standardized test findings has led some school administrators and teachers to follow textbook prescriptions and thereby regiment instruction without further consideration of individual learner needs.

Second, in some school situations an overemphasis has been placed on the adequacy of standardized tests for measuring the reading facet of language development. For example, a test over word recognition and paragraph meaning is used sometimes as the only basis for identifying reading needs. A careful study of the many highly interrelated factors in reading ability should soon dispel such notions regarding the adequacy of certain standardized reading tests for appraising the many specifics in reading ability.

Third, some administrative and supervisory officers appraise the [reading] instructional programs only by means of standardized test data. In fact, some go so far as to post on the school bulletin boards the class averages that advertise the so-called effectiveness of the teacher. Instead of acting as a spur to better teaching, some "wise" teachers will use copies of standardized tests for instructional purposes, thereby invalidating the findings. In these situations, vicious procedures are the result. These misuses of test materials lead to still other unfortunate outcomes. The authors of these tests tend to become dictators of the [reading] instructional program; both teachers and pupils tend to develop fears of standardized tests;

and the more important goals of pupil development are neglected and not achieved. (Betts, 1946, p. 441)

As a result of this unfortunate situation Betts succinctly notes that in some cases,

...the test is the sole criterion for evaluating the teacher! (p. 25)

Throughout his professional career, Betts (1941b) emphasized that the solution to overdependence on standardized reading testing is the competent teacher's use of informal forms of assessment.

It is satisfying to note that many progressive and alert teachers are resorting to subjective tests and informal situations for determining the level of achievement in reading. It has been found, for example, that very few, if any, standardized tests can be used for determining the level at which instruction in reading should begin. When dealing with elementary school pupils, a competent teacher can determine the level of achievement for practical purposes more quickly by observing behavior on the materials or problems in question. (p. 39)

Reader's Background Knowledge and Experiences

In this passage, Betts (1943) speaks to the teacher, especially about the teaching of content reading, who believes that meaning resides on the printed page rather than as an outgrowth of each student's unique background experiences. Memorizing facts and information only is not understanding.

Teachers in all subject matter areas can improve their instruction through a better understanding of pupil development in the reading facet of language. In learning situations, language and facts cannot be divorced. When pupils are required to memorize dates in history, the "meanings" of lists of words for "vocabulary development," terms in science and the social studies, and the like, a first-class group of verbalizers is produced. Verbalism, or sheer wordiness, results when language is overemphasized. To insure meaning for the learner, vocabulary and the other aspects of language must stand for, or represent facts within the learner's experience. In a so-called reading class, the development of verbalization is all too likely to result. Then, again, the teacher who is bent on getting facts across to a class in a laboratory situation may neglect language development, especially the reading facet of language. As stated by E.L. Thorndike (1934, p. 3), "...words and constructions should be learned in association with, and subordination to, facts and principles." In a well-balanced [reading] instructional program, each teacher assays the potentialities of learning situations for their contributions to pupil control over language-fact relationships. (Betts, 1943, pp. 37–38)

Oral Reading

In many classrooms today, students still can be found sitting in small groups reading orally to the teacher in round-robin fashion. This meaningless oral reading is usually done without prior opportunity for first reading the material silently. In the following passage, Betts (1943) clearly notes the impropriety of this practice and gives sound reasons for first reading the material silently.

[S]ilent reading should precede oral reading. A corollary to this may be stated; the silent or oral rereading should be motivated by purposes (i.e., problems or questions) different from those which governed the preceding silent reading. Directed silent reading before oral reading has at least four merits: first, each child in a group can read without having his performance paced by another child. Second, silent reading permits the learner to identify and to overcome specific comprehension and word recognition difficulties. Third, the oral rereading may be done with facility; that is, without the reader's being hampered by comprehension or mechanical problems. Fourth, the pupil is

given an opportunity to make maximum use of word
recognition skills, especially context clues. (Betts, 1943, p. 39)

Reading as a Thinking Process

The reading process is clearly a cognitive process of the highest order; yet unfortunately, many classroom reading programs are based on the belief that teaching reading should involve learning isolated skills. In the following passage, Betts (1962) notes the critical importance of effective thinking as the basis for all reading activities.

Teaching pupils how to think is a major goal of reading instruction. But available evidence demonstrates that pupils who have not learned how to think in reading far outnumber those who have not learned essential skills. The thinking facet of reading instruction is based on four fundamental considerations:

First, reading is thinking that results in comprehension. In reality, reading materials are concepts, not word forms— concepts of time, space, cause, self, and so on. These concepts are organized personal experiences made by the pupil. Understanding and recall of these concepts are strongly influenced by his attitudes; for example, his attitude toward segregation of peoples, communism, military service, et cetera. Furthermore, straight thinking is required for drawing conclusions from related facts, cause-effect relationships, and analogies.

Second, reading is thinking in a language. Pupils know a foreign language or the language of mathematics when they can think in it. Therefore, to learn how to think in English, they study systematically the relationships between parts of sentences, use of levels of abstraction (e.g., iron-metal-mineral), punctuation, use of definite and indefinite terms (e.g., three feet versus near), different meanings of a root (e.g., cour of courage) or an affix (e.g., ful of careful), figurative language (e.g., mountains of potatoes), idiomatic language (e.g., to beg the question), shifts of meanings of words (e.g., root of a plant, to root around), et cetera.

Third, reading is a relationship with the author. Communication between author and reader is more than literal interpretation of what the author says; that is, sponge-type reading. Hence, pupils are taught to ask these questions: Why did the author write on this topic? What does he want me to do? What do I think about what he says? What use can I make of his ideas?

To answer these questions the pupil learns to do critical, or depth, reading and creative reading. He is on his way to becoming an independent thinker in a free society—capable of detecting those who rush past a basic question of issue. There is hope that he will be no mugwump reader hypnotized by the magic of clichés.

Fourth, reading is the use of skills for a specific purpose. To become an efficient, versatile reader, the pupil learns to skim directions, dictionary entries, indexes, tables of contents, chapter headings, and to locate ideas. But equally important, he can shift to power, or depth reading to separate facts from opinion, to evaluate the relevance of an idea to this purpose, to organize ideas, and to draw valid conclusions. (pp. 7–8)

Grade Level and Reading Achievement

Achieving grade level by all students in reading is often the standard used to judge whether a classroom or school reading program is a success or a failure. As Betts notes in the following selection, the use of grade level as an effective measure in determining reading success is frequently not reflective of real achievement in reading. Unfortunately, despite statements such as these by Betts (1941a), significant effort continues to be made on making grade-level achievement the ultimate determining factor in the supposed success or failure of a school's reading program.

The use of the term "grade placement" undoubtedly has been a most significant psychological barrier to clear thinking in regard to schools. Erroneous ideas regarding grade placement [in reading] have caused teachers to send parents a vicious type of home report (report card), to regiment children in their classroom activities, to misuse and invalidate graded instructional materials, and to otherwise violate what has been learned by the scientific study of individual differences. Parents, too, have fallen into fallacious thinking regarding "grade placement." They have been taught to believe that all children upon entrance to first grade should be taught to read, and that a report card should be an infallible and desirable report of the pupil standing in a class rather than a report of individual progress, that all children of a given class should progress through the same book at the same rate. Children have been the victims of false identifications and invalid abstractions.

In some modern schools, the use of the term "systematic sequences" has been found to be one way to direct thinking and, therefore, practice away from entrenched concepts of "grade placement." The use of the term systematic sequences implies that learning is systemic and an individual matter. The teacher of a given "grade" who concerns herself with the systematic learning sequences of her pupils finds herself unable to rationalize regimented instruction in which all the children do the same thing at the same time. She capitalizes on the wide range of capacities, abilities, interests, experiences, and drives. No longer does she evaluate an individual's progress in terms of "average" class achievement or pace his progress by the calendar through a prescribed course of study. Instruction begins where the learner is. Needs are determined cooperatively by the teacher and the learner. What is to be learned is no longer kept a secret by the teacher and assigned to the class on a page-by-page basis. Many undesirable tensions are removed and individual progress is not paced by the class average. A grade becomes a group of children who learn to live in terms of democratic processes. (Betts, 1941a, p. 42)

Motivation for Reading

To develop an interest and desire to read in all students is of utmost importance in the development of lifelong readers. Effective classroom teachers can do much to encourage students to see reading as not only a school subject, but rather as an important part of their lives. Betts (1941a) provided suggestions on how to improve student motivation in various reading activities.

> Reading is a thinking process, therefore the development of adequate reading habits should contribute to clear cut and organized thinking. This means the learner must know the purpose of the reading. Recreational reading in school should lead the pupil to make "worthy use of leisure time." Information type reading should develop skills, abilities, and attitudes to make the learner adequate for solving certain problems through reading. Hence, the learner should be motivated to read for the purpose of answering his questions or solving his problems. The activity assumes importance to the learner and gives direction to his behavior to the extent that it has immediate value to him.
>
> The practice of having a pupil read the next page or the next paragraph never has been recommended in professional publications, yet it appears to be an entirely too common practice. This hearing of lessons by an unprepared or a disinterested teacher has stifled interest in school activities and has done much to contribute to retardation in reading. Basic reading skills and abilities—location of information, selection, evaluation, organization, comprehension—must be developed in functional reading situations. If the situation is functional, then it has meaning and value to the learner.
>
> Adequate motivation should provide the learner with information regarding the validity of the materials and of the developmental [of related] activities. Handing a book to a child and telling him to read has proven to be one of the weakest forms of motivation, because it has no intrinsic meaning to him. It probably is an excellent procedure for developing word callers. On the other hand, children have been known to work

long hours on a reading project when motivated from within. Preparation for a dramatization of the organization of a report lends validity to reading materials. (Betts, 1941a, p. 41)

The Total School Reading Program

In a powerful summary statement, Betts (1936) set a standard against which a school's reading effort can be measured, even today. Note especially the opening and closing statements about the basic roles of teachers and of reading.

All teachers are teachers of reading. Arithmetic, social studies, music, and science offer excellent opportunities for the acquisition of reading skills. One of the chief dangers of a departmentalized or platoonized elementary school is that of compartmentalization where subjects are emphasized rather than children. The recent tendency to eliminate school readers has forcefully called attention to the need for a definite program of reading and study in all school activities.

In the past, reading has been regarded too much as a drill subject. In the first place, reading is only a tool and not a subject to be studied as such.... From the very beginning, reading should be a part of an activity where the pupils want to learn something in particular; that is, reading should be taught from the reading-to-learn point of view.... (p. 16)

It is also erroneous for the teacher to have the philosophy that reading instruction should be given only during the reading class. If reading difficulties are to be prevented, each teacher must assume the responsibility for furthering practice in situations where reading is involved. If everyone looks to the so-called reading teacher to do the task, reading deficiencies are certain to persist because there are specific reading skills and information which can be taught functionally only through activities connected with the content subjects. Every teacher should be a teacher of reading. (pp. 242–243)

REFERENCES

Betts, E.A. (1934). *Bibliography on the problems related to the analysis and correction of reading difficulties.* Meadville, PA: Keystone View.

Betts, E.A. (1936). *The prevention and correction of reading difficulties.* Evanston, IL: Row, Peterson.

Betts, E.A. (1941a). Correction of reading difficulties. *Visual Digest, 5*(1), 39–44.

Betts, E.A. (1941b). Basal readers. *Visual Digest, 5*(2), 38–45.

Betts, E.A. (1943). Specific reading needs. *Visual Digest, 7*(2), 34–44.

Betts, E.A. (1946). *Foundations of reading instruction.* New York: American Book Company.

Betts, E.A. (1962). Updating reading instruction. *Education, 83,* 3–10.

Betts, E.A., & Betts, T.M. (1945). *An index to professional literature on reading and related topics.* New York: American Book Company.

Thorndike, E.L. (1934). Improving the ability to read. *Teachers College Record, 36,* 1–19.

Reflections

Emmett Betts was particularly interested in the role of the classroom teacher in encouraging students to see reading as a lifelong experience. Consider how you might apply Betts's thinking in your own classroom literacy instruction.

1. Betts suggests several primary goals of an effective reading program. Based on his ideas and your own, what would you like your students to accomplish each year in reading? Name specific ways in which you might accomplish these goals in reading.

2. Although Betts identified and discussed problems related to the use of standardized tests, oral reading problems, and grade level expectations in reading over 50 years ago, many of these problems still exist today. How do you deal with these issues in your current classroom reading instruction?

FURTHER READING

Betts, E.A. (1936). *The prevention and correction of reading difficulties.* Evanston, IL: Row, Peterson.

This important early reference discusses diagnosis and remediation of various reading difficulties, with particular emphasis on the fact that most reading problems are the result of a variety of problems and not, as commonly thought at that time, one single cause.

Betts, E.A. (1946). *Foundations of reading instruction.* New York: American Book Company.

This basic literacy textbook is considered a landmark reference used to train numerous generations of elementary classroom teachers in the techniques of teaching reading skills. The contents reflect Betts's belief in the importance of the teacher as primary factor in the effective classroom reading program.

Cassell, R.N. (Ed.). (1971). Dr. Emmett Albert Betts: Teacher, publisher, writer, author, founder. *Education, 91*(3), n.p.

This article provides an excellent overview of Betts's life and work.

[Reading research] clearly shows that a large proportion of children who are considered "unteachable" may learn to read when adequate diagnostic and remedial steps are taken.

The questions posed by a teacher—before, during, and/or after reading—have greater influence on growing reading competence than any other single procedure used.

It seems clear to me that if an attitude of inquiry is fostered and if the techniques of critical thinking are taught, this ability may increase throughout life as background and experience develop ever more higher standards against which to judge what is read.

Not only is the ability to learn to read of major significance, but the ability to learn through reading is paramount in most content areas.

Helen M. Robinson (1906–1988)

*H*elen M. Robinson was a national leader in reading education for many years. As a graduate student at the University of Chicago (Chicago, Illinois, USA), she studied with William S. Gray (see page 17 in this volume), working primarily in the area of reading disabilities. Her dissertation research, published as *Why Pupils Fail in Reading* (1946), established that most reading problems result from a multitude of causes rather than a single cause as previously believed. This interdisciplinary model has been used often by researchers and is considered a classic in the literacy field.

During her tenure at the University of Chicago, Robinson was responsible for the development and implementation of a number of innovative programs. She organized and directed the Reading Clinic, which was one of the first at a major university. The clinic was designed to diagnose young people with reading problems, as well as to train clinicians for the public schools. Because of its success, this clinic model was replicated throughout the country in a variety of universities and public schools.

Of particular importance was Robinson's leadership in forming the annual Reading Conference held at the University of Chicago. Organized in 1937 by Gray, Robinson was director from 1953 through 1961. The Reading Conference was one of the most important literacy meetings held during this period, due to the quality of both the presenters and the topics that were discussed. The proceedings from the conference, published under Robinson's direction from 1953 to 1961, are considered some of the most important literacy publications in the history of reading education.

Robinson's publication and professional record was extensive and varied, and included most notably the editorship of the *Annual Summaries of Investigations Relating to Reading* (1960–1969), and the National Society for the Study of Education's yearbook, *Innovation and Change in Reading* (1968). In 1961, Robinson was appointed the William S. Gray Research Professor in Reading at the University of Chicago and held this position until her retirement in 1968. She was also one of four original members of the Reading Hall of Fame and served as the first president of the International Reading Association. Helen Robinson's contributions to the field of literacy education, particularly in the area of understanding disabled readers, have been of lasting importance.

Excerpts From the Writing of Helen M. Robinson

The Role of Effective Teaching and the Treatment of Reading Disabilities

In the following passage, Robinson (1946) notes that although the diagnosis of reading difficulties is important, it is secondary to effective reading instruction. She also notes that merely identifying reading problems (calling them "anomalies" in the following selection) is insufficient without the use of appropriate teaching strategies. Even today, with the emphasis on "quick fixes" for solving reading problems, the importance of the effective classroom reading teacher must be reemphasized, as Robinson suggests.

> Many of the anomalies in allied fields may be discovered and remedied without appreciable growth in reading. This is because such remediation only prepares the child for learning to read and does not teach him the skill. A direct, vigorous reading program must follow correction of causal factors. For example, correcting a visual difficulty does not teach the child to read, but enables him to learn with greater ease when he is given remedial instruction. Likewise, psychiatric treatment for an emotional problem results in no reading growth without teaching, but it may remove the emotional block so that the child is able to direct his attention toward learning. In many instances it is probable that an enthusiastic, capable teacher can motivate a child to learn to read, even though he has inhibiting difficulties, although much less time and effort might be needed if the inhibiting factors were corrected prior to learning.
>
> Efficient and flexible techniques for teaching reading are extremely important, especially to children whose inhibiting difficulties cannot be readily corrected. (pp. 236–237)

Current Practices in the Teaching of Reading

Today, as in the past, reading education often is the focus of criticism by the general public. Although the response from reading educators to criticism takes many forms, most often it has been to quickly adopt unproven methods and approaches. In the following passage, Robinson (1961) addresses this seemingly unending problem, suggesting that it is the informed classroom teacher who makes the difference.

The teaching of reading has been the target of public criticism intermittently since the advent of public education. During the last decade, a more vehement phase of criticism has placed many administrators and teachers in a position where they were forced to defend their procedures. In the process of defense, many found it necessary to reexamine curriculum and practices and to search for new ways to meet the needs of children and youth. These circumstances have provided a natural setting for experimentation in teaching reading. Public interest has encouraged change, leading to innovations in organizing classrooms and in methods of instruction.

Change in teaching, for its own value, may only provide a temporary impetus to better teaching. Therefore, careful and continuous evaluation of the results of different plans of organizing the classroom, different methods of teaching, and different materials is essential....

A casual glance at the records of the use of reading by today's citizens is unimpressive. Again and again teachers, librarians, and parents ask what is being done to promote intelligent use of reading. Obviously, then, we cannot be satisfied with the status quo. We need to make bold strides, but we must be sure of their worth, if we are to improve the reading competency of our future citizens.

Eagerness for improvement in teaching reading is not to be interpreted as condemnation of past practices. Instead, nothing in life has been done the way it should be; the world is full of all sorts of things to do over and do right. The foregoing statement is attributed to Lincoln Steffens, but it applies today as well as in the past. We are all aware that children have never learned to read and to use reading as well as they might. But when we "do it over" we must be sure that we "do it right."

New plans, new techniques, new books, new gadgets, and other panaceas for teaching reading are the rule rather than the

*exception today. Enthusiasm for each reaches great heights with
some teachers and, of course, with representatives who sell each
program. The administrator who is pressed to improve his
curriculum, or the conscientious teacher who wishes to develop
greater reading competence among his pupils, may be sold on
these new departures without fully weighing the evidence for or
against their adoption. Some writers have found it impossible to
examine controversial issues critically; they seem to be unable
to use reason rather than emotion. (pp. 1–2)*

Remedial Reading Programs and the Classroom Teacher

The use of reading specialists is a common practice in today's schools.
Most often these teachers work with individual or small groups of students, apart from the regular classroom. Robinson (1953) addressed
this special staffing arrangement, noting both positives and problems.

*Throughout the years of the development of remedial reading
programs, the research and practices [of these programs] have
influenced classroom methods in the teaching of reading. The
extent of this influence probably cannot be measured, but the
directions in which it has operated appear to be both
constructive and destructive. On the positive side, case studies
of individuals who were successfully tutored have emphasized
the need to appraise reading readiness; to develop various
phases of readiness prior to beginning reading instruction; and
to explore visual, auditory and emotional functions of
beginning readers. Successful remediation has demonstrated
the need to adapt reading materials to the learning level of each
pupil rather than to rely upon a single textbook in each grade.
Remedial reading instruction has lost its reputation of being
magical so that many of its methods are easily adapted to
classroom instruction. The study of severely retarded readers
has revealed that numerous problems develop because of
prolonged failure. As a result, school personnel are urged to
identify retarded readers early and to institute corrective
measures before serious retardation develops. Case study*

methods have been adapted for classroom use to encourage the teacher to secure a better understanding of pupils.

Unfortunately, other effects have also been revealed. In some schools a remedial reading program has been instituted as a substitute for a developmental reading program. In those instances, classroom teachers have ceased to assume any responsibility for reading instruction. This trend was cited in the Proceedings of the Third Annual Reading Conference when Gray (1940) stated: "Many schools...have become so deeply absorbed in improving the status of poor readers that most of their constructive effort in the field of reading has been directed to diagnosis and remediation" (p. 2). In fact, in some schools, reading is systematically taught to all pupils only through third, sixth, or eighth grade. This plan is based on the assumption that pupils who read satisfactorily will continue to make progress with incidental guidance while those who fall behind will be taught by the remedial teacher. This assumption has already been recognized as a serious error in school planning, with the result that there is a changing concept of the function of the remedial reading teacher. In many schools this teacher is now called a "reading consultant," and his responsibility is to assist classroom teachers by making diagnosis, providing suitable materials, demonstrating appropriate teaching methods, and generally assisting with an in-service teacher training program.

Another practice which has often proved to be ineffective is assigning remedial reading classes to teachers who, for one reason or another, are ineffective in the classroom. Without any preparation or materials, these teachers frequently fail to obtain positive results. A similar practice is to assign a remedial reading class to any English teacher who will accept it in high school or college. Quite often such a class is reassigned each year because the teachers, without training in this area, find no satisfaction in dealing with the retarded readers. Thus the classroom teacher is relieved of the responsibility of meeting the needs of the poor reader, and, at the same time, no constructive plan is instituted in the special class. (Robinson, 1953, pp. 12–13)

The Best Approach to Teaching Reading

From the beginning of reading instruction, teachers have been searching for the best or the perfect approach to teaching reading. Even today, this seemingly endless quest is evident in the fervor associated with the adoption of each new reading philosophy or approach. In the following selection, Robinson (1969) addresses this search for the perfect reading method. Her remarks are particularly relevant for today's reading teachers because we are still criticized by many (for example, politicians, the media, and the public) for not using a particular system or approach to teach reading. In the following passage, note the reference to the First-Grade Reading Studies, which as Robinson notes, clearly established the fact that there is no one best way to teach reading. The results of this important reading research need to be recognized by more classroom teachers.

Reading instruction in the primary grades needs careful scrutiny. The importance of early success to later achievement has been shown by a number of studies [Bloom, 1964]. It seems axiomatic that the best teachers are needed at the beginning. It is especially important that the teachers be flexible and able to use a variety of approaches rather than attempting to fit children to a single approach.

Methods for teaching beginners has been the topic of heated arguments, both inside and outside the profession. When defensible solutions to this problem were not forthcoming, the U.S. Office of Education supported the largest cooperative research project ever undertaken to compare a large variety of beginning reading methods. In their report from the center that processed all of the findings, Bond and Dykstra [1967] concluded that no single method was distinctly superior in all situations and that there was no "best method" (p. 35). Perhaps the best method for the greatest number of children depends on the strength of conviction of the teacher that a given method is most effective. If so, Bond and Dykstra's advice to pay more attention to teachers and the learning situation may be the best policy for future planning.

The accumulated research demonstrates very convincingly that several approaches to beginning reading may be offered to young children rather than relying on any single approach as has been the usual practice. Teachers of beginners should profit by acquaintance with a number of approaches to reading. Moreover, these teachers can operate far more effectively if they can diagnose early problems and reteach immediately to prevent prolonged failure. The time has long passed when giving all children "more of the same" is justified, either by research or by experience. Likewise, pacing of pupils' progress through the early stages of reading will surely vary with the learning rates of children. (Robinson, 1969, pp. 35–36)

Content Reading in the Middle Schools

A current reading problem of major concern is those students who reach the middle grades and beyond and are still having reading difficulties. Robinson (1969) addressed this issue, noting specific ways in which the content teacher can help these struggling readers.

It is unfortunate that by the middle grades many teachers appear to believe that all children have learned to read and henceforth will read to learn. Less flexibility to individual and group differences than in the early grades often are practiced, but the needs are fully as great. Even though the time available for teaching reading is reduced by additions to the curriculum, adaptations must be made if all pupils are to continue to make progress.

In addition, the content of printed materials believed to be appropriate for these years is less familiar and further from children's experiences. The vocabulary increases markedly, especially in the different content areas, as does the variety of language patterns. If earlier emphasis has been placed on learning the cues to solving words and on determining what the author said, at the middle-grade level emphasis may properly be placed on identifying the cues to the message the author meant to convey. Too often this aspect of understanding is neglected at the middle-grade levels....

[I]f continued instruction in learning to read accompanies reading to learn, growth in both aspects appears to be enhanced. Many pupils still need help with decoding and continuous emphasis on the variety of meanings of many words is crucial as these words are met in new contexts. Most children should attend to literal comprehension of passages of increased difficulty and complexity. In preparation for competency in independent reading, pupils should learn to determine the relevance of different selections to a given topic; this ability requires them to read several sources, to summarize and synthesize. From these few examples of expectations it should be clear that teachers will profit from using a variety of sources rather than just a single textbook for their reading instruction. Another implication is that assignments, guidance and questions asked must go beyond the factual level which requires only direct recall. Dealing with this type of question calls for more time and interchange of ideas than is needed for reproducing a statement from the text. Often unequivocal answers cannot be given so that the teacher guides the discussion to arrive at the best consensus, demonstrating the kind of reasoning and the selection of evidence to support one answer in preference to another.

[E]mphasis should be placed on rational judgments about materials so that pupils will develop the foundation for critical reading. No longer can we afford to have children, even in the middle years, say "I know it is true because it says so in the book." Children need encouragement to question many statements and conclusions in books, newspapers, magazines, and other sources. Indeed, every teacher should expose children at this level to different versions of the same event or situation and to guide in using available resources to judge accuracy and worth of each source so as to arrive at defensible conclusions....

[R]eading in each of the content areas is an essential part of the developmental reading program in the middle years. There is general consensus among experts that the attitudes and skills are taught best along with the content. However, teachers find it difficult to divide their attentions between teaching the *curricular knowledge to be acquired in science or social studies and the reading of the materials. Consequently, the suggestion is made that, periodically or as needed, the reading lesson include the appropriate way to read arithmetic problems, science, and other texts because reading periods tend to concentrate on literary materials. Such instruction might include a study of vocabulary, symbols, maps, graphs, time charts, patterns of thinking (inductive, deductive), and the appropriate rates of reading in each area.*

[A]s in the earlier levels, instruction should continue to include personal reading, not incidentally but as an integral part of the program. Some children will choose to read science fiction, science magazines, or other informational materials. Others will choose to read fiction. All pupils need access to a wide variety of books which satisfy their interests and needs. Individual conferences about personal reading have proven to be a tremendous motivating factor [Sartain, 1960], as they demonstrate that the teacher places high priorities on the use of reading as well as on learning to read better just to score higher on end-of-the-year tests. (Robinson, 1969, pp. 38–39)

The Mature Reader

The ultimate goal in reading is to develop the mature reader. Unfortunately, today, although illiteracy rates (numbers of people who cannot read) are a great concern, aliteracy (those who choose not to read) is a relatively unexplored area. In this passage, Robinson (1960) summarizes the characteristics of the mature reader.

The mature reader, according to Gray and Rogers [1956], has a focus which motivates him to turn to reading. This interest causes him to search for selections which further illuminate his understanding or enrich his personal and social life. For this purpose he actively seeks books, magazines, newspapers, and other resources. Because of his background, he is searching for particularly relevant titles; he is alert and ready to appraise the competence of the author to write the book or article, then either he rejects it or delves into it. In the latter case, his purpose is to appraise the relevancy of the content to the topic in which he is interested. He is likely to read the introduction and skim the remainder, stopping at particular points to read more carefully. Finally he may read the conclusions; then he decides whether or not he wishes to spend further time in reading the entire book or article. If he chooses to do so, his purpose for reading is clearly defined but different from the previous one. Now he wishes to read carefully and appraise the message so that he automatically selects the proper rate and adapts the level of inquiry to the materials at hand. Ideas are acquired instantaneously as the reader's eyes cover the words, which are no longer units to recognize but triggers to thought. As Gray and Rogers (1956) said, "reading at this top level of maturity loses its quality of vicariousness and speaks directly to the reader" (p. 237). In the process of getting the author's meanings, he stops to reread a sentence to get the full import or to note the beauty of expression. He may even drop his book a moment to reflect. Suddenly he says to himself, "I see," which means that a new concept has joined the many he already possesses.

The mature reader's search for knowledge or insight, or the solution to a social problem, has caused him to concentrate on securing the author's message. To communicate with this author, the reader has run the gamut of the various aspects of reading, maintaining flexibility in his emphasis....

Thus the mature reader can move flexibly from meaning to language, emphasizing one aspect or another of reading because he has thoroughly mastered each of the processes required to read in this manner. The skills in recognizing words and the attitude of constant search for meaning are automatic. (p. 238)

REFERENCES

Bloom, B.S. (1964). *Stability and change in human characteristics*. New York: Wiley.
Bond, G.L., & Dykstra, R. (1967). The cooperative research program in first-grade reading instruction. *Reading Research Quarterly, 2*, 115–142.

Gray, W.S. (Ed.). (1940). *Reading and pupil development* (Supplemental Education Monograph No. 51). Chicago: University of Chicago Press.

Gray, W.S., & Rogers, B. (1956). *Maturity in reading.* Chicago: University of Chicago Press.

Robinson, H.M. (1946). *Why pupils fail in reading.* Chicago: University of Chicago Press.

Robinson, H.M. (1953). Problems of corrective reading in American schools. In H.M. Robinson (Ed.), *Corrective reading in classroom and clinic* (Supplementary Educational Monograph No. 79, pp. 12–13). Chicago: University of Chicago Press.

Robinson, H.M. (1960). The unity of the reading act. In H.M. Robinson (Ed.), *Sequential development of reading abilities* (pp. 237–244). Chicago: University of Chicago Press.

Robinson, H.M. (Ed.). (1961). *Controversial issues in reading and promising solutions* (Supplementary Educational Monograph No. 91, pp. 1–2). Chicago: University of Chicago Press.

Robinson, H.M. (1968). *Innovation and change in reading instruction. The sixty-seventh yearbook of the National Society for the Study of Education.* Chicago: National Society for the Study of Education.

Robinson, H.M. (1969). Future reading instruction. In J.A. Figurel (Ed.), *Reading and realism* (Vol. 13, Part 1) (pp. 33–41). Proceedings of the Thirteenth Annual Convention of the International Reading Association. Newark, DE: International Reading Association.

Sartain, H.W. (1960). The Roseville experiment with individualized reading. *The Reading Teacher, 13,* 277–281.

Reflections

Consider the following questions as they relate to the writings of Helen Robinson.

1. Do you agree or disagree with Robinson's belief about the basic role of the classroom teacher in the diagnosis and treatment of reading difficulties? What do you see as successes and difficulties in dealing with various reading problems in your classroom?

2. Do you agree with Robinson's definition of a mature reader? How can you help your students develop maturity in their reading activities?

FURTHER READING

Robinson, H.M. (1946). *Why pupils fail in reading.* Chicago: University of Chicago Press.

This book is considered a classic reference in the diagnosis and remediation of reading difficulties. It clearly shows that reading problems are almost always the result of a number of causes.

Weintraub, S. (1994). Helen Mansfield Robinson. In M.S. Seller (Ed.), *Women educators in the United States, 1820–1993.* Westport, CT: Greenwood Press.

This essay, written by one of Robinson's colleagues at the University of Chicago, is an excellent review of her life and work, particularly her professional work at the university.

[I]t follows that a modern program in reading deals not only with reading skills but with more general competencies, interests, tastes, and effects of reading on the child.

There is little disagreement among either philosophers or psychologists about the close relationships between language and most thinking.

Basic reading programs are one of the school's most potent influences upon child development.

[The teacher of reading today] is beginning to inquire less often, "What is Johnny doing in reading?" than "What is reading doing to Johnny?"

The responsibility of the school to help develop clear-thinking individuals rests on at least two principles: (a) the ability to think critically begins in early childhood and develops slowly, and (b) the school curriculum offers many opportunities for clear thinking, especially in various types of reading activities.

David H. Russell (1906–1965)

*D*avid H. Russell was an important educator not only because of his research and writing in reading education, but because of his work related to language and thinking. His book *Children's Thinking* (1956) is considered an important reference in this aspect of cognition. Throughout his writing, Russell returned repeatedly to the theme of the importance of language, especially as it relates to children's reading and thinking.

Russell's professional career included roles of classroom teacher, elementary school principal, and professor at the University of Saskatchewan (Saskatoon, Canada) and University of California at Berkeley (California, USA). He served as president of the National Council of Teachers of English from 1962 to 1963, and as president of American Educational Research Association from 1958 to 1959.

Author of many articles and books, Russell's most well-known works about reading were *Children Learn to Read* (1949) and a series of classroom-oriented materials that included *Listening Aids Through the Grades* (1949) and *Reading Aids Through the Grades* (1938).

Of special interest is Russell's research and writing on the effects of language on the reader. Although it may seem obvious that reading would have either a positive or negative effect on the reader, relatively little research had been done on this subject before Russell's work. Much of David Russell's research on children's thinking and the effects of reading on their personality development was important during his lifetime and still has implications for reading teachers today.

Excerpts From the Writing of David H. Russell

A Summary Statement on Reading

In the following passages, Russell (1951) discusses the qualities that make up an effective classroom reading program. He clearly emphasizes the fundamental importance of meaning as the foundation for successful reading. Note what he says about the role of the mechanics of reading, especially related to phonics and oral reading. Of particular importance are his comments about the social setting for reading and the classroom teacher's role in promoting this idea. Although written 50 years ago, Russell's views about teaching reading have much to say to reading teachers today.

Paramount goals to be gained from reading are meaning, comprehension, and the understanding of ideas and their communication.

Communication is a two-way process. It means receiving ideas from others and giving ideas to them. In reading, these two activities are self-evident to any experienced teacher. As the child reads, he gets ideas from the printed page if they are associated with his previous experiences, and he gives ideas to others in reading orally or in telling or writing something of what he read.

In other words, reading is not just the receiving or absorption of ideas. The silent reading act is complete only when the reading is put to use in some way, and this usually means communicating with others in discussion, reporting, summarizing, interpreting, or recording.

If a teacher or school staff accepts the dictum that reading is largely concerned with the two-way communication of ideas, there are at least three inferences which can be made regarding curricular practice.

Stimulating Ideas

First, if reading is largely concerned with the communication of ideas, the teacher's first task is the stimulation of ideas. In one sense, reading is not so much getting ideas from the printed page as bringing ideas to it. The child can interpret the abstract symbols of a sentence, paragraph, or chapter only as he has experience which enables him to interpret these symbols.

We can read only as we have a rich background of experience related to the concepts, pictures, or related forms presented in print. This has long been recognized as a principle of reading readiness. In preparing children to learn to read, the school is concerned largely with the building of experiences such as practice in oral language, picture interpretation, storytelling and listening, following directions, and working in a small group, all of which are necessary background experiences for reading. Understandings, plus some ability to communicate one's understandings, are prerequisite to initial reading success.

The work the teacher and children do together before the children open their books may be the most crucial phase of the reading lesson. In this phase the teacher, assisted by the children, sets the stage. Here the children get some clues to the theme of the story or selection, certain difficult concepts are presented and clarified, and then the children are given some specific purposes for reading the selection silently. Upon the stimulation of ideas will depend the success of the whole directed reading lesson.

In the larger sense, success in any type of reading depends upon the store of ideas and purposes the children have in relation to that reading. In schools where children have chances to observe, manipulate, visit, experiment, and construct, they are building up ideas and purposes for reading. This is the school's initial task if the children are to be successful readers.

Getting Your Ideas Across

Second, if reading is largely concerned with the communication of ideas, the mechanics of reading are important only as they contribute to clear communication.

In the struggle to provide for the needs of 25 or more very different individuals, no teacher can be blamed for losing sight of the larger goals of reading....

It is equally true, however, that word recognition and other skills need to be subordinated to understanding ideas. Research indicates that an emphasis upon meaning or ideas in teaching is more profitable than a continued emphasis upon mechanics. Where children have a chance to reach for important or exciting ideas, their reading abilities, including the mechanical skills, improve most rapidly.

One of the chief disadvantages of the older type of phonetic training was that it continually confronted children with such gems as, "The fat cat sat on the mat." After meeting such ideas for weeks, who would want to learn to read? The modern contrast is the young child who eagerly turns the page for more interesting, even exciting, ideas.

It seems clear, then, that in the teaching of reading the skills should remain subordinate to the meaning. The child should be asked to develop word recognition skills such as using the sounds of initial consonants, noting the effects of the silent e or syllabizing only that he may grasp ideas readily and coherently. If he has to stop and laboriously work out a word for himself, usually he will have lost the meaning of the sentence or paragraph. That is why, in the developmental reading lesson, the teacher quickly tells the child a word he fails to recognize. After the meaning of the selection has been determined and discussed, it may be necessary to go back to work on the difficult word or words, but such work must never interfere with grasp of meaning or enjoyment of a story.

All children develop mechanical skills in reading, but we must beware of thinking that these are important in their own right. They are simply keys to unlock doors leading to comprehension of a rich variety of ideas.

Social Setting for Reading

Third, if reading is largely concerned with the communication of ideas, many reading activities must emphasize communication in a social setting. Skillful teachers emphasize the communication aspects of reading by providing situations in which important ideas are transmitted.

The day when we used to think of reading as entirely an individual skill, to be practiced alone as much as possible, has largely gone. It is true that children who have books accessible will always use reading for personal enjoyment and recreation, but it is equally true that some of the enjoyment in books comes from sharing their ideas with others. Accordingly, from the first grade onward, the teacher plans situations in which reading operates as an exchange of ideas.

This emphasis upon the communication of ideas means that the teacher will use "oral reading around the circle" sparingly if at all. Even in the first grade the children are asked to turn over their books to listen while June reads about what the Red Hen did next or what Tom said. In the first months of

school the teacher often says, "Listen while Catherine reads the
chart story so you can tell...."

 The social setting or reading is important at all school
levels. If children are to be encouraged to listen, of course they
must usually be asked to listen to ideas that are new or fresh to
them. Hence it is important to introduce "audience reading" of
new books, fresh stories, or individual selections brought home
by one child for the rest of the group to enjoy. The ideas read
should often be valuable for carrying on related activities. The
functional reading of directions for work, announcements,
problems, and plans for next steps are examples which
emphasize the communication aspects of reading. Any busy
classroom presents varied opportunities for true audience
reading. (Russell, 1951, pp. 274–276)

The Effects of Reading on the Reader

David Russell was interested in learning about the effects of reading
on the reader. The following selected passages show the development of
his ideas on this topic, from a general lack of knowledge about it to
specific suggestions on how classroom teachers can help students to see
reading as a positive influence in their lives.

 Studies in the effects of reading are the present no man's land in
the language arts area. Since at least the 1880s, starting with
Javal and Cartell, the psychology of the reading act has been
charted with considerable care. Beginning a little later, the
problems of reading behavior and instruction have been
explored and analyzed by Buswell, Dearborn, Gates, Gray,
McKee, Thorndike, and by their students and other workers. It is
in the third area, the investigation of the effects of reading, that
large unknown regions and unmapped territories exist today.

 The volume of research in the psychology and teaching of
reading is attested in many tests and in summaries such as
those of Betts, Traxler, and Witty. Gray's annual summaries of
worthwhile reading studies currently include about one
hundred items each year.

Betts's bibliography [Betts & Betts, 1945] listed 8,278 studies and articles up through 1942, and the flood has continued almost unabated since then. A search of those sources, however, reveals practically no mention of serious investigation of the effects of reading. We know what eye movements in reading are like, the probable causes of reading disabilities, how children attack new or partly known words, some reasonable expectancies for reading abilities as children progress through school, but we don't know the results or effects of their reading. Can reading good books counteract living in a slum? Are the comics as bad as some people say? What happens to a child when he reads a fairy tale? Does a tale of courage help a timid child to develop some courage of his own? These and many other specific questions about the effects of reading remain largely unanswered.

There are valid reasons for this neglect of an important area. The teacher concerned with 30 or even 35 children necessarily concentrates on the process, not the product. She and the children in the group are happy [if] Jim makes no mistakes on his page or if Jake learns one difference between long and short vowels. In the busy day there isn't too much time for reading in relationship to values and ideals or to mysterious needs. So too with the principal. The score on the reading test may count heavily here. Even the school psychologist, who may have considerable insight into the effects of reading on personality, is often called in only to diagnose difficulties and outline a program of remedial instruction. Parents are not trained to look for deeper effects, librarians are busy keeping up with the new books, and school people are necessarily occupied with some of the more obvious results of their reading program. (Russell, 1954, p. 335)

Today teachers are beginning to emphasize the effects of reading on children. Some personal values of reading and literature develop in individual situations but others depend upon the individual as a person in a functioning group. A boy's reading is something like his ambition to own a bicycle. At first *he wants it for its own sake, for the personal pleasure and for the feeling of having acquired something new. But later he uses his bicycle to visit his friends, to become better acquainted with his community, to do errands such as carrying messages in a larger circle of acquaintance. So with reading. Emphasis upon the communication aspects is important for its own sake, but even more it will contribute to the wider socialization of the child. (Russell, 1951, p. 277)*

Russell (1970) summarized the possible effects of reading into four main categories. Although similar to those of other writers, Russell's list of possible effects summarizes the research of many other writers. This type of listing should bring to mind numerous opportunities to encourage a wide range of student response to various types of literature.

Possible Effects of Reading

Instrumental

1. *Enrichment of experience.*
2. *Acquisition of knowledge, facts.*
3. *Increased understanding of human relationships.*
4. *Encouraged writing of imitation activities (dramatic).*
5. *Encouraged reading of the same or different authors.*
6. *Increased abilities in reading (general).*
7. *Resulted in greater liking (for animals, and so on).*

Reinforcement

1. *New or changed attitudes.*
2. *Helped general personality adjustment or development of philosophy.*

Respite

1. *Identification with character or characters.*
2. *Enjoyment of fantasy.*
3. *Wish fulfillment.*

4. Escape and relaxation.

Esthetic

1. Enjoyment of humor, adventure, romance.

2. Appeal to imagination.

3. Application of character.

4. Enjoyment of illustrations.

5. Portrayal of arousal of emotions.

6. Literary appeal (criticism, rhythm, vocabulary, and so on).
(Russell, 1970, pp. 275–276)

A Healthy Personality and Reading

In the following selection, Russell (1952) discusses six ways that classroom teachers can help students develop healthy personalities through reading. Note how the problems he identified in 1952, such as an insecure world, possible negative effects of mass media, and family-related problems still face young people today.

1. *If you believe reading can influence personality, plan ways to increase chances of identification and projection. Let us look beyond reading as an intellectual exercise to reading as a process involving emotional responses, empathy, and therapy. Let's give 12-year-old Bill a chance, through reading, to be Red Wilson and score the winning basket with 10 seconds left to play, but let us also give him the chance to show moral courage with the fictional hero's defense of a boy from a minority group. Let's make discussion of character and values a part of many reading experiences. Such discussion and sociodrama may lead to desirable identification.*

2. *If you believe that reading may develop self-insight, you will probably work on the assumption that a good book of fiction interprets life more clearly than a didactic book. If you believe that the imaginative rather than the prescriptive writer has the power to describe and project to*

the reader some phase of personality, then you as the teacher will enlarge the recreational phase of your reading program. Here in so-called library books the purposes of reading include establishment of permanent interests in literature. But they go beyond habits to where the child, freed of the necessity of finding the right answer, the one right answer, may gain that self-insight which is one mark of the well-adjusted person. In developing self-insight, the resources of biography may be tapped more than they have been. Many of the modern biographies for children and youth combine fact and fiction to give the struggles and conflicts of others as a mirror in which one's own problems can be viewed clearly and profitably. Such examples of life-writing give youth a chance to share the strengths of a Schweitzer or Gandhi and to know a weakness as in Stephen Foster's sense of the unworthiness of his own music. Most biographies have action and suspense; the life of a scientist can compete with modern science fiction or even Space Cadet. In recreational reading of this sort lie many chances for the development of self-insight, one phase of the healthy personality.

3. If you agree that the child faces insecurity in a troubled world and that he often has no close-knit group of his own, you can use reading as an aid to security and belongingness. Most of you know one or two children who over-use reading as compensation for insecurity at home or in the peer group. There may be dangers in much reading for a few children, but for the majority reading can be a socializing influence. As they enjoy a story together under the teacher's guidance, most children feel they really belong to the group. As they read of others who are isolated or rejected, they gain the feeling that they are not alone. Reading can add to their feelings of security and belongingness. Group work can be planned with this aim in mind.

4. *If you agree that the children or youth you know best live in a confused world, you can help them develop their values, the things they live by. The schools are one of the few places where youth can evaluate critically the emphasis upon swank or the fast buck of the typical Hollywood movie or the desire for the many possessions fostered by the slick magazines. Through reading, discussion, and sociodrama, children can be helped to see that there are high motives and low motives, selfish answers, and socially valuable solutions. The current crop of sports stories for adolescents often poses directly the problems of sportsmanship versus win at any cost, building a decent life versus athletic glory or financial rewards. From the primary grades onward, reading plus action can reveal some of the ethical values which the child or youth must acquire in our schools if he is ever going to get them.*

5. *If you agree that the child is often over stimulated by the modern media of mass communication, you can plan reading periods for relaxation and escape. The escape can be in the quiet humor of Pooh and Homer Price or the mild adventure of Cowboy Tommy or Johnny Tremain. Radio and television won't often provide that relaxation. Their programs are paced to keep your attention so you won't turn off your set. There must never be any "dead air." In contrast, teacher and child can use the leisurely paced story. Every teacher should read something to his class everyday. Sometimes this can be a quiet story for a quiet period such as the leisurely approach of* The Wind in the Willows *[by Kenneth Graham]. You remember, for example, the description of how Mole felt after his day on the river with Rat:*

> *This day was only the first of many similar ones for the emancipated Mole, each of them longer and full of interest as the ripening summer moved onward. He learnt to swim and to row, and entered into the joy of running water; and with his ear to the reed-stems he*

> *caught, at intervals, something of what the wind went*
> *whispering so constantly among them.*

Time to hear what the wind is whispering! In this feverish, over stimulating world, reading is one of our last resorts for the quiet times which are one resource of every healthy personality.

> *6. Finally, if you agree with the sociologists that the American family is in danger of dissolution, if you feel that home and school can do much together in building the healthy personality, you will help the child with his reading. The day is gone when the teacher can ignore the parent's help in reading and other areas. The home is usually not the place for instruction in specific techniques in reading, but it is the place for building up permanent habits and interests in reading. Many of you are now discussing children's literature at PTA's and other parent meetings and taking advantage of National Book Week each fall. You are encouraging use of the public library, sending home notices of new books at school, and encouraging the use of vacation reading lists. Are you thus contributing to the healthy personality? Of course. The healthy personality is one in which the person has achieved a set of rewarding habits and interests. With opportunities for identification, for increasing security and belongingness, with chances for relaxation and for enriching ethical concepts, all these with the habit of reading will help develop the healthy personality.* One of the alphabet rhymes in the *New England Primer* was

My Book and Heart
Must never part.

Books and hearts can still be close together! (Russell, 1952, pp. 197–199).

REFERENCES

Betts, E.A., & Betts, T.M. (1945). *An index to professional literature on reading and related topics.* New York: American Book Company.

Russell, D.H. (1949). *Children learn to read*. Boston: Ginn.

Russell, D.H. (1951). Reading as communication. *Childhood Education, 27*, 274–277.

Russell, D.H. (1952). Reading and healthy personality. *Elementary English, 29*, 197–199.

Russell, D.H. (1954). Unsolved problems in reading: A symposium I. *Elementary English, 31*, 335–338.

Russell, D.H. (1956). *Children's thinking*. Boston: Ginn.

Russell, D.H. (1970). Possible effects of reading. In R.B. Ruddell & D.H. Russell (Eds.), *The dynamics of reading* (pp. 275–276). Waltham, MA: Ginn-Blasidell.

Russell, D.H., & Karp, E.E. (1938). *Reading aids through the grades*. New York: Teachers College, Columbia University.

Russell, D.H., & Russell, E.F. (1949). *Listening aids through the grades*. New York: Bureau of Publications, Teachers College, Columbia University.

Reflections

David Russell was interested in the relationship between reading and its effect on readers. Consider the following questions relating to his works:

1. Russell provides specific ways in which wide reading can have positive effects on student reading. In what ways can you implement Russell's ideas in your own classroom reading program?

2. What problems must you overcome in order to implement these ideas in your classroom reading instruction

FURTHER READING

Ruddell, R.B., & Russell, D.H. (Eds.) (1970). *The dynamics of reading*. Waltham, MA: Ginn-Blasidell.

> Although this book was completed after Russell died, it is an excellent statement and summary of his interest and research on the effects of reading, especially as it relates to the use of wide reading.

Russell, D.H. (1949). *Children learn to read*. Boston: Ginn.

> This is an important textbook on the teaching of reading, and it clearly reflects the author's philosophy of reading with specific implications for classroom implementation.

Russell, D.H. (1956). *Children's thinking*. Boston: Ginn.

> This book is considered a landmark reference in the study of children's thinking, and is particularly strong in its review of existing research and work in this area.

On one point parents and teachers agree: Most youngsters want to read and they all need to read. That ability is required of them for good living in our modern world. The person who cannot read is frustrated at almost all levels. We depend on reading for our jobs, our information, and our pleasure. We literally read to live.

Real reading means plucking out all the subtle threads of meaning from sentences, paragraphs, and pages and weaving them into your personality.

So skills, skills, skills! We must distinguish between skills, which there are some in the act of reading, and thinking abilities, of which there are a great, great many.

Growth through reading is the ultimate goal of all instruction, while growth in reading is the means to that end.

A. Sterl Artley (1907–1998)

A. Sterl Artley was a prominent reading educator most noted for his work in the area of teacher training and development in reading instruction. While a faculty member at the University of Missouri-Columbia (Columbia, Missouri, USA), Artley was instrumental in organizing one of the first reading clinics based on the concept of knowing the total child. As clinic director, Artley emphasized that a child's ultimate reading performance is based on a number of factors, including home background, physical condition, and past educational experiences. This successful model of reading diagnosis, based on a complex view of reading disability, was duplicated in many other clinics.

As an early president of the International Reading Association, Artley's leadership was most evident through his writing on the importance of the well-trained, experienced classroom teacher as the essential foundation of an effective reading program. His scholarship is most noted for the continual emphasis on the fact that no one preferred approach or technique in reading has proven superior to all others.

Artley wrote extensively on the role of sound-symbol relationships, or phonics, in an effective reading program. He was also coauthor of a number of commercial reading instructional materials, including the "Dick and Jane" series of basal readers.

If one conclusion can be drawn from Artley's lifetime work in literacy, it is that quality reading instruction is, in the final analysis, balanced teaching in all its various aspects.

Excerpts From the Writing of A. Sterl Artley

Unfortunately, in some reading programs, classroom teachers become so absorbed in the details of teaching a specific program or approach, they simply forget that reading should be an experience that enriches children's lives. In the following passage, Artley (1955b) clearly establishes that meaningful reading is much more than just learning isolated skills.

The Purpose of Reading

[For classroom teachers of reading], there must come the growing realization that, as important as growth in reading power may be, such growth is significant only in so far as it

enables the child to enrich his experiences and to grow personally and socially. Reading has served its highest purpose when through it children become better, stronger persons. To achieve this end, reading must "come alive" for the child. It must be a medium through which he experiences richly, as richly as if he were actually taking part in the story. Achieving this goal of personal development requires that children learn to project themselves into story situations; to share the characters' moods and emotions; to create vivid sensory images of sight, sound, movement, touch, and smell. And, because the child lives richly the content he reads, he comes to formulate guiding principles that he uses in his own personal and social life. In this manner the child is not only taught to read, but also, through reading to live. (p. 6)

Diagnosing Reading Difficulties

Today, schools are faced with an increasing number of students in middle and high school who have serious reading difficulties. What may seem to be a recent problem is in reality one that has plagued educators for some time. Artley (1940) suggested reasons why the problem existed then and how it might be solved effectively. Despite the fact that he wrote this material over 60 years ago, note how timely it sounds and how little change has taken place in the years since.

Reading in the Content Areas

With the increased attention to the various aspects of reading in the primary grades, there has come about in the last decade a growth of interest in the problem in the secondary school. The situation confronting the two school levels are not analogous, however. In the primary grades there seems to be little doubt as to the aims to be attained, or as to the techniques to be used in attaining these aims. On the other hand, though a very definite reading problem is recognized on the secondary level, neither the aims nor the techniques are so well recognized or defined. We have not yet come to a conclusion as to whether the high school should concern itself with remedial reading for those with reading handicaps, or whether it should attack the problem on a broader front with reading treated as a distinct school subject....

Our first concern must be an attempt to come to an understanding as to the place that reading shall occupy in the secondary school. To be more specific, shall we emphasize remedial reading for a few, or reading for all? The answer that we shall get to this question depends upon the point of view we take toward reading in general, whether in the primary or secondary grades.

The point of view or philosophy of reading, which has vitally changed our teaching techniques and instructional methods in the grades, is that reading is essentially an adjustment to be made rather than a skill to be acquired. As we shall try to point out, this philosophy not only affects our activities in the grades, but it gives us a definite basis upon which to construct our program in the secondary school....

As a result of a gradual but inevitable evolution, brought about by research and experimentation in psychology and related fields, the emphasis today is on reading-to-learn rather than learning-to-read. Stated in another way, our fundamental beliefs in relation to the function of reading are based pretty much upon the common-sense answer to the simple question, "Why do we read, anyway? To call words, or to get meaning?" Hence our materials and methods were changed drastically, and now the first graders are reading their charts and primers primarily to get the meaning of an interesting and coherent story. True, in acquiring the meaning, the children are also learning to recognize words, but their prime concern is in interpretation and enjoyment. Hence they read to enjoy a story; they read to learn how to make a birdhouse; they read to learn how butter is made. They read to learn. Reading, then, in its broadest terms is not a subject to be learned, but a tool that has new uses and applications as new situations arise. It is an adjustment to a new situation. (Artley, 1940, pp. 47–48)

Oral Expression and Background Experience

In the following passages, Artley (1953) stresses the importance of the relationship between oral expression and reading development. In the first paragraph, he defines the reading process and emphasizes its importance in relation to a reader's background experience.

Oral Reading

A child can read no better than he can organize his ideas and express them. This generalization is rooted in a principle basic to the psychology of reading. Reading is a process of thinking, interpreting, and reacting. Printed symbols serve only as triggers to release the thought-process, to set it in action. Since the thought-process cannot take place in a vacuum but must deal with ideas already in mind, the importance of comprehending, organizing, and using ideas on a spoken level is readily apparent. Too often we are inclined to think of reading as a subject to be taught—sounds, syllables, and skills—rather than as a process of interpreting and reacting, the basic elements of which are laid down in oral language.

Since interpreting and reacting to printed symbols is only a short step removed from interpreting and reacting to spoken symbols, the need for attention to oral-language growth is of primary concern. When this fact is overlooked, many children are in the position of having to attach meaning to a printed symbol when the symbol lies outside their spoken vocabulary; to understand a printed 10-word sentence when normally they speak only a disjointed three-word sentence; to interpret a complex sentence when they have difficulty in using simple ones; to follow the organization of a new story that they are trying to read when they are unable to tell in logical order the events in the familiar "Little Red Riding Hood"; to read complete sentences with expression when they are unable to give emphatic expression to their own ideas; to interpret punctuation marks when they attach no significance to gestures, pantomimes, and free play. Truly, we are asking many children to place the cart far, far ahead of the horse. (p. 321)

Teaching Phonics Skills

Among teachers of reading, there is no more controversial subject than that of phonics. Issues abound on how phonics skills should be taught, the appropriate materials and techniques to be used, and whether phonics has a place in an effective classroom reading program. In the following material, Artley (1955a, 1979) discusses the history of the phonics controversy and what constitutes a good program of phonics instruction.

Of all the issues facing teachers of reading, it is safe to say that none is so controversial as that of word perception, and we might add, so surrounded with emotional overtones. In the last 2 decades there have been a number of articles written on the subject. Because in many cases the issues and the basic assumptions behind them have not been clear, much of the writing has resulted in confusion rather than clarification....

Word Perception and Goals of Reading Instruction
The first issue has to do with the relation of the word perception program to the overall goals of reading instruction. In question form we would state it as follows: What part of the total reading program shall be given over to the teaching of sight words and to the development of independent techniques of word perception?

A point of view implicit in a number of reading programs is that instruction in word perception is the most important part of the program. In fact the teaching of reading is the teaching of word recognition, with only a modicum of attention directed to other goals of instruction. Consequently, we find much of the program given over to word drill, word games, separate phonics periods, and word recognition activities divorced from functional reading. A great deal of the instructional material is unrelated to story content, being made up of lists of words and nonsense syllables used for the purpose of drill.

This type of program is characterized by a certain supplementary phonics drill book of some 125 pages where only a total of 8 pages is given over to connected (?) discourse.

Though presumably built for the primary grades, the drill words that are supplied are those that are completely foreign to the vocabulary of a typical primary child. In fact, one word isn't even in the dictionary. Another program, almost exclusively phonics in nature, claims that a first grader can be taught to recognize words commonly found on fifth-grade word lists. By the amount of drill material provided, and the recommended amount of time the teacher is supposed to give these materials apart from reading, the validity of this claim would not be doubted. But what virtue is attached to an average first grader learning to pronounce fifth-grade words? What a terrific price we ask children to pay for their whistle.

The opposing point of view holds to the idea that the word perception program is merely a part of the total reading program—an important part, let there be no doubt about that, but a part that serves as a means to interpretation rather than as an end of reading instruction. This point of view is held by Gray and others who conceive of the total interpretative act as being made up of the identifiable components of word perception, comprehension, reaction, and integration. Word perception is then a part of the total act of reading.

This being true, the word perception program must be closely integrated with the reading act, not set apart in separate instructional periods, nor handled through extraneous drill materials. The words from which recognition principles are inductively derived are those the child has met in his daily reading. As he acquires a new perception skill, he applies it directly to new words which he meets in his daily reading. Emphasis throughout is on interpretation, with perception skills serving that end. Otherwise, the reader runs the risk of being able to "phonics his way through any word," but unable to derive or to react to the author's meaning.

Content of Word Perception Program
The second issue I should like to discuss has to do with the content of the word perception program. In what areas shall we attempt to develop word perception skills and abilities? On this

issue the lines are clearly drawn between those who would limit the program to a single area, namely phonics, and those who would advocate the development of abilities in several areas, such as context, structural analysis, and the use of the dictionary.

Within the last year [1954–1955], in several popular magazines, articles have appeared extolling the merits of the phonics approach to reading instruction. One of the writers contends that the teaching of reading is simple. Since reading means getting meaning from certain combinations of letters, all the teacher needs to do is to teach the child what each letter stands for and he will be able to read. He adds that this is the "natural system" of learning to read, and that the "ancient Egyptians...the Romans...Germans...Estonians...and Abyssinians" learned to read that way.

Though we may smile at these broad and sweeping generalizations, there are those who believe that a return to the methods and content in vogue at the turn of the century would be the solution to all our reading problems. The number of so-called "phonetic systems" on display at the bookstands at professional meetings is mute testimony to the belief of many in the philosophy of the old oaken bucket.

The point of view most widely accepted by reputable reading people today—Gates, Gray, Witty, Durrell, Betts, and others—is that phonics is merely one of several methods that the child may use to unlock words. This contention gets its strength from basic research done in the late 30s and early 40s by Tate, Tiffin, and McKinnis, Russell, and others who conclude:

- *Phonics is only one method of word recognition.*
- *Phonics instruction should be closely integrated with purposeful reading.*
- *Though intensive phonics instruction may improve ability to recognize words, it makes little contribution to silent reading comprehension.*

There is not a series of basic materials on the market today that does not include instruction in phonics, but it is functional phonics, not a superimposed system of reading. It is closely integrated with meaningful reading, and taught in close conjunction with other procedures such as context clues, structural clues, and word-form clues. The basis for this practice rests in the following assumptions:

- *English is a language that follows no lawful pattern of pronunciation as German or Spanish. Consequently, no single method of word attack can be depended upon. This becomes increasingly obvious as the reader meets more involved polysyllabic words.*

- *Whereas one can sound out simple three- and four-letter words with only a minimum loss of time, one's rate of perception is slowed down materially as he attempts to use a highly synthetic approach on more involved words.*

- *Since meaning is the primary consideration, those devices which give the child clues to meaning as well as to form are of primary value—hence, the importance of context clues, structural analysis (emphasizing root elements, prefixes, suffixes, inflectional endings, etc.), and the dictionary.*

True independence in reading is attained when the child can with dispatch and confidence, unlock any word he meets on his own terms, be it short or long, simple or complex.

The Teaching of Word Perception Skills
The last issue I propose to discuss is somewhat related to the preceding one. Assuming that we are committed to the development of a versatility of word attack by equipping the child with skills, abilities, and understandings in several methods of word perception, the question then arises as to how this program shall be carried out. Shall one begin by teaching the sounds of the elements, leading eventually into the synthesis of the word whole from known components, or shall

one begin with sight words, withholding until later the teaching of analytical procedures?

A writer in one of the popular articles to which I have already alluded would begin his program by teaching the sounds of the letters. He says, "As soon as you switch to the common sense method of teaching the sounds of the letters, you can give them a little primer, and then proceed immediately to anything from this magazine to Treasure Island [by Robert Louis Stevenson]." Let us examine this contention critically. Reading is the process of creating meaning from word symbols. It must be a meaningful experience, an interesting, vital experience. But what meaningful experience can be associated with the sounds of m, or b, or st, or any other auditory or visual component? Possibly the most important thing the teacher can do with beginning children is to help them develop a favorable attitude toward reading. From the time she begins, reading must be an interesting, pleasurable, meaningful experience. It is difficult to see how the teaching of meaningless, discrete sounds or elements, and "doing phonetic gymnastics" can go very far toward developing this essential attitude.

Those who understand that potency of motivation in the learning process insist that the initial contact with reading be through meaningful words, perceived as wholes, not as parts. Because the child's concern is with the meaningful unit he comes to see that reading is fun—a pleasurable experience. Some would take issue with me on this point and say that we need not be concerned with making reading fun. They contend that children might as well learn early that learning to read is a matter of blood, sweat, and tears. Yet, I will defend to the last the point that unless children see early that reading is an avenue to new and exciting experiences they are not going to turn to it in their free time nor use it as a source of information. They will become the avid readers of comic books and viewers of television. They will also be the ones who haunt the reading clinics because they see no point and purpose to an uninteresting activity.

Phonics Should Be Functional

As I have already pointed out, there is a place for phonics as well as other procedures of word perception, but they should not take precedence over the primary function of reading which is to create meaning. They should be introduced after a basic stock of sight words has been established. This basic stock of sight words serves two purposes: first, that of developing desirable attitudes toward reading; and second, that of providing the stock-in-trade for the inductive development of generalizations about sounds, endings, prefixes, similar and dissimilar elements, etc. After these principles have been developed from the basic stock of sight words, they may then be applied to new words. It seems to me this is sound psychology.

Furthermore, research shows that a typical child should have a mental age of 7 before phonics generalizations can be meaningfully learned and applied. As a result, much of this work is reserved for the second year and beyond. However, this does not preclude a rich and meaningful program in readiness for phonics and structural analysis. Of course, it is during this time that the basic stock of sight words is being developed. (Artley, 1955a, pp. 196–199)

Once reading begins, one of the most important instructional tasks is developing competencies of word identification. From the days of the Horn Book the assumption has been that word identification is the process of turning printed symbols into spoken words and spoken words into meaning. Because words are made up of letters which stand for sounds, the act of word identification becomes that of "sounding out." This "sounding out" required teaching all the letter-sound relationships along with the "rules" for determining the sounds for which letters stood, particularly vowels, as they occurred in words.

Primary teachers know from experience that the teaching of phonics is not only a laborious process for both teacher and pupils but one having limited value. Research shows that there are so many exceptions to the so-called phonics rules that the process becomes trying and confusing. Clinics and special reading programs are filled with children who can sound out the words but still can't construct meaning.

Furthermore, psycholinguists point out that readers, young children included, bring to the reading act a group of understandings inherent in oral language which, when used for the identification of unfamiliar written words, make unnecessary the sole dependence on phonics.

First, children are aware that words must go together in a prescribed order. Though they may be unfamiliar with the rules of syntax, they know they must say, "The frightened boys hurried back to the tent," rather than, "Tent boys the back frightened hurried the to." They need no formal instruction on parts of speech to come to this conclusion. They "know" that adjectives precede nouns and that nouns precede verbs. Children know also that it would not make sense to read, "The fried boys hurried back to the tent," or "The frightened boughs hurried back to the tent."

Thus words must both fit the structure of the sentence and make sense. Such concepts about language, intuitively acquired in the process of learning to talk, may now be applied to the identification of unfamiliar words in the act of reading.

In meeting the sentence, "Jerry sat down on the _____ to his house," the reader asks, "What word would fit and make sense in the sentence?" The word steps seems to meet both criteria, but the reader might conclude that the words walk or porch would also fit.

A third understanding about words that the teacher will help children generalize is that words must also conform to the spelling-sound (graphophonemic) pattern of the word; a word beginning with st eliminates porch and walk. Note that the reader did not "sound out" the unfamiliar word but combined three bits of information about language. Since so many words begin or end with consonants, simple graphophonemic information about consonants eliminates the necessity for learning and applying unreliable phonics rules.

In developing the strategies to be used in the identification of unfamiliar words, the teacher must permit, in fact encourage,

*the reader to take chances, to try out various possible words
until one is found that meets the criteria: "fit, sense, and
sound." "Read to the end of the sentence," the teacher suggests,
and "see if you can figure out what the word must be." The
teacher is asking the child not to randomly guess, but to infer on
the basis of known language understandings.*

*In discussing strategies for identifying unfamiliar words,
one might ask, "Just how important is it that the reader come up
with the identical word that that author used?" If in the sentence
above, the reader thinks* home *for* house *or* porch *for* steps,
*have unpardonable reading errors been committed? Neither of
the substitutions would change the inherent meaning of the
paragraph—about a problem Jerry is trying to resolve. Meaning
is the important consideration in reading—not word
pronunciation! (Artley, 1979, p. 15)*

The Role of the Teacher and Reading

While most educators would agree that it is the role of the classroom
teacher that is the critical element in an effective reading program, this
fact is often lost in the continual search for the "perfect" reading materials or most effective method of reading instruction. In the following ex-
cerpt, Artley (1981) stresses the fundamental importance of the teacher
as the basic foundation of all good reading programs.

The Teacher as a Factor

*After all has been said and done, there is still strong evidence to
show that it is not the method, the materials, the approach, or
the room arrangement which make the major difference in
pupil adjustment and achievement. Though the approach or
materials may affect student reading achievement, in the final
analysis, it is the teacher who has the greatest effect. This not
surprising fact was brought out in the First Grade Reading
Studies [Bond & Dykstra, 1967], which attempted to determine
if there were differences in reading achievement that could be
accounted for by different methods and materials. On the basis
of this comprehensive experimental study the authors
concluded that it was what teachers did in their relation with*

children that made the major difference in reading achievement. This fact was dramatized by the discovery that frequently there were greater differences in pupil achievement between teachers using the same method than between teachers using different methods....

Individualize or Personalize

The fact that it is the teacher and his insightful manner in dealing with children that makes the major difference in achievement, changes somewhat one's perception of the merits of approaches to [reading] instruction, whether the approaches deal with materials, programs, or provisions for individual differences.

    It is in the connection that Gillian Cook in a recent article in Language Arts *[1981] differentiates between the teacher as an artisan, "skilled in manipulating the tools of the trade, assisted by skills tests, pre-packaged 'teacher proof' materials and modern technology," and the teacher as an educator "who can facilitate children's healthy growth and development in ways that will enable them to live successfully in our complex society" (p. 51). It may appear that such a concept of a teacher, when applied to the area of reading, is so vague and ambiguous that it fails to give teachers a sense of the direction instruction should take. One must hasten to point out, however, that such a concept of the reading teacher's responsibility does not negate in any way the importance of the acquisition of reading competencies. Assisting the child to become a competent reader requires the same degree of attention to specifics as does development of writing or speaking ability. However, the added dimension in reading is that the competencies must be developed in such a way as to make them functional. To be specific, if the teacher is developing the concept of sequence of events, that concept needs to be used in searching out the sequence of events in a story or whatever is being read. Or, in developing the skills involved in using an encyclopedia, students must actually be required to use an encyclopedia. In short, competencies being developed need to be applied functionally lest they become useless.*

Along with all that is involved in teaching is the overriding need for the competent and effective teacher to personalize instruction. Based on his knowledge of the subject area with which the teacher is dealing, the psychology of how children learn, the effect of learning styles, the influence of motivation, and an awareness of societal expectations, the teacher amalgamates these various elements into a teaching style which makes teaching, and hence learning, a personal matter for each child under the teacher's direction. In this manner a teacher personalizes rather than individualizes instruction.

It is hoped that teachers and administrators will realize that no reading program will solve all reading problems. Teachers must creatively adjust any reading approach to the needs and responses of the students whom they teach. (Artley, 1981, pp. 149–151)

Teaching Suggestions for Effective Reading

In the following four statements, Artley (1980) summarizes his beliefs about what effective reading teachers do in their teaching. This advice was based on a lifetime of experience and teaching in the field of reading education.

First, make unstructured independent reading a major component of your instructional program. For it is as children actually read that they will have the opportunity to employ the competencies acquired, but even more, that they will come to experience the pleasure of reading. Whether learners are in a developmental or remedial situation, they must see reading as a personally rewarding experience rather than as a pointless task.

Second, use your instructional time for silent reading rather than oral, with teacher questions that give the readers an opportunity to think about and react to what they have read. Give children a chance to develop their reasoning abilities in the real context of reading rather than through practice exercises.

Use questions that permit alternative responses and discussion, for out of such activity children come to see the difference between careful and uncritical thinking.

Third, the learning process involved in acquiring any ability is an individual matter. Some children will need much more time than others to acquire concepts. Don't require the practice of a rule for the child who has generalized the rule already and has discovered the rule irrelevant to reading. Engage in teaching activity for those who need it. Let the others read.

Fourth, in spite of what I have said about drill activities, I know that many teachers will continue to use them. This being so, give children an opportunity to go over their practice responses with you. Observe how a child's thought processes led to a particular answer. This will give you a chance to review or reteach as the occasion demands. Remember, a practice exercise is a teaching device, not a test. (Artley, 1980, p. 21)

A Primary Goal for Reading Instruction

Reading often is considered by teachers to be a skill to learn in much the same manner as those skills found in mathematics or science. Artley (1940) disagreed with this view of the reading process, noting that reading should be considered an avenue for all learning rather than a separate subject. As you read the following passage, think of both the philosophical and the practical changes that might occur in reading instruction if this idea were implemented in a typical reading curriculum.

As a result of a gradual, but inevitable, evolution brought about by research and experimentation in psychology and other related fields, the emphasis today is on reading to learn rather than learning to read. Stated in another way, our fundamental beliefs in relation to the function of reading are based pretty much upon the common-sense answer to the simple question, "Why do we read, anyway? To call words, or to get meaning...?" Reading, then, in its broadest terms is not a subject to be learned, but a tool that has new uses and applications as new situations arise. It is an adjustment to a new situation. (p. 48)

REFERENCES

Artley, A.S. (1940). Guidance in reading for the few or all. *Education*, *61*, 47–48.

Artley, A.S. (1953). Oral-language growth and reading ability. *The Elementary School Journal*, *53*, 309–328.

Artley, A.S. (1955a). Controversial issues relating to word perception. *The Reading Teacher*, *8*, 196–199.

Artley, A.S. (1955b). Some "musts" ahead in teaching reading. In *Reading for today's children. Thirty-fourth Yearbook. The National Elementary Principal*. Washington, DC: Bulletin of the Department of Elementary School Principals, National Education Association.

Artley, A.S. (1979). The word is psy'-cho-lin-guis'-tics. *School and Community*, *65*, 14–16.

Artley, A.S. (1980). Skill overkill. *School and Community*, *66*, 18–21.

Artley, A.S. (1981). Individual differences and reading instruction. *The Elementary School Journal*, *82*, 147–151.

Bond, G.L., & Dykstra, R. (1967). The cooperative research program in first-grade reading instruction. *Reading Research Quarterly*, *11*, 5–142.

Cook, G. (1981). Artisans or educators: The NCTE statement on the preparation of teachers of language arts. *Language Arts*, *58*, 51–57.

Reflections

As you reflect on the writings of A. Sterl Artley, the following questions should help you sum up his basic views of the reading process, particularly the role of the classroom teacher in an effective reading program:

1. Based on Artley's beliefs about the sound-symbol relationship and the effective role of phonics in the reading process, how do they compare or contrast with your teaching of these skills?

2. Artley defines reading as being "an adjustment to a new situation." What do you think this phrase means, and how might you adjust your classroom reading instruction to meet this goal?

FURTHER READING

Artley, A.S. (1953). *Your child learns to read*. Chicago: Scott Foresman.
> This book was written for parents to explain the learning processes their children go through as they learn to read. Many suggestions are included on how parents can help their children become better readers.

Artley, A.S. (1968). *Trends and practices in secondary reading. A review of the literature*. Newark, DE: International Reading Association.
> This is an excellent review of the knowledge base of teaching reading as it relates to content instruction. Although the title indicates "secondary reading," the implications would apply to middle grades as well.

There is no better tonic for stimulating interest in a [reading] task than recognized success....

The relative emphasis on phonics has waxed and waned through the years, but heavy doses of it were no panacea for reading failures.

Only when the teacher sees reading as a dynamic interaction between the personality of the reader and literature will her influence grow beyond a mechanical drilling of skills.

[Effective reading instruction]...may also be achieved by abandoning rigid standards of progress in the first three grades. Progress should be a continuum rather than a series of distinct steps. Pupils will be permitted to progress at their own rate and will be given varying amounts of time to complete the primary program.

George D. Spache (1909–1996)

*R*eading difficulties have long been of concern to educators, and George D. Spache was a leading authority in the diagnosis and correction of these problems. He is most noted for his work with disabled readers and for development of both formal and informal reading assessment measures. The most well known is the Spache Diagnostic Reading Scales (1980), which consists of a series of integrated reading tasks that include oral and silent reading, as well as auditory comprehension. This individually administered test was widely replicated and set the standard for the informal diagnostic measure for many years. Spache is also known for his work in the area of text evaluation, especially the development of the Spache Readability Formula (1953). Spache's professional writing was wide and varied, from general textbooks on teaching reading to those more specialized, dealing with analysis and correction of reading disabilities. Of particular interest to Spache was the relation between reading disability and vision problems. At the University of Florida (Gainesville, Florida, USA), he established one of the first child study clinics devoted primarily to reading problems. His writings based on his work there have made an important impact on the study and remediation of reading disability.

Throughout his professional career, Spache was noted for frankness and candor in both his professional writing and speaking. He believed that the best way to deal with problems in the field of reading education was to be forthright about possible solutions. Although other educators may not have agreed with Spache, they certainly were clear about his views and beliefs.

Excerpts From the Writing of George D. Spache
Schools as a Causation of Reading Difficulties

George Spache's candor and directness about issues was never more evident than in the following discussion about the role of schools and teachers as a possible cause of reading disability. Most educators do not want to think that their efforts may lead to reading problems in students, but that is Spache's (1976) message in the following passage. The passage begins with several questions about issues related to schools and reading disability, then describes the positive reading status of many students when they begin school, and asks why they eventually develop reading problems.

Is it conceivable that competent and well-meaning teachers actually create cases of retardation among their pupils? Is it true that many pupils become retarded in reading simply because of what happens or fails to happen in the classroom? Are the majority of reading failures free from obvious handicaps in vision, hearing, intelligence, personality, and the like? Many experienced reading clinicians and supervisors will probably give an emphatic affirmative answer to these questions. Moreover, the statistics emanating from remedial programs of all types point an accusing finger at classroom practices as causes of reading failure. Diagnosticians find relatively few children for whom the obvious cause of retardation is found solely in physical or psychological areas. The majority of retarded readers are normal or average in these causal areas, or, at least, they were normal in most respects during the early stages of reading instruction. What happens in classrooms to cause almost one out of every four pupils to fall seriously behind his age group at some time during his school career? (p. 129)

A Teacher's Definition of the Reading Process and Its Effect on Students

Spache (1976) described some teachers' beliefs about the reading process not by what they said, but rather through their various teaching activities. The passage begins with a definition of these beliefs, then lists a variety of classroom teaching practices based on these beliefs. Most effective reading teachers would seriously disagree with most of these practices, but they probably know fellow educators who nevertheless include such practices in their current reading instruction. Sadly, although these comments were written in 1976, they apply to many reading teachers today.

We consider her [the teacher's] concepts of the [reading] process of paramount importance, for they influence every aspect of her instructional practices. To the average primary teacher and to many at intermediate grades, the process that she is teaching the children is the pronouncing of printed words, learned largely through repetition, with some assistance from phonic, structural, and contextual clues. She demonstrates this concept of the process of learning to read in many ways such as these:

1. *Daily oral reading lessons in a circle emphasizing almost exclusively correct recognition of words.*

2. *Vocabulary exercises making no distinction between words that are meaningful and those that function only to give structure to sentences.*

3. *Flash cards and other exercises that drill on all types of words out of context.*

4. *Questions emphasizing immediate recall of the words just read to the exclusion of interpretation of the thought.*

5. *Drill on letter sounds and letter combinations in isolation from words or in relatively meaningless words.*

6. *Practice in phrase reading from cards displayed at far-point, as though the span was similar to that at reading distance.*

7. *Judgment of progress of children based largely on their success in reading orally, that is, in pronouncing words.*

8. *Emphasis upon oral reading as though it were similar to, or foundational to, silent reading.*

9. *Slavishly leading pupils through each successive page of the material in the belief that this practice controls the number of new words and that the vocabulary offered is fundamental to future reading.*

10. *Coaching on new words at the chalkboard prior to actual reading for fear that the initial misreading of these words would prevent their eventual learning. (Spache, 1976, pp. 125–126)*

The Role of Methods and Materials in Reading Failure

In the following passage, Spache (1976) directs his attention to the dominant role of materials and methods in the "typical" classroom reading program. Note his candor in this discussion.

The American classroom teacher commonly bases her instruction on some set or group of commercial instructional materials. Each such piece embodies a concept of the process of learning to read, and a continuum of skills development that will guide both teacher and pupils toward the authors' objectives. Each reading skill is practiced to a degree in keeping with the authors' emphasis upon it as a basic part of the process of learning to read. No one really knows what the most effective skill sequence is, nor whether all the skills taught are essential for most children to read. But all these plans are offered [to] groups or total class instruction, as though they were the best possible system for most or all pupils. As a result, the average tends to employ a system or method of teaching reading without really questioning its relevance to the individual differences among her pupils.

The fact that some reading methods are based on, let us say, unique or esoteric definitions of the reading process is often ignored. To some, learning to read is a matter of first learning the sounds of individual letters or letter combinations and then blending these sounds into words in isolation or in patterned sentences that keep repeating certain combinations of sounds in almost meaningless phrases. To others, learning to read is the process of associating printed words with common meaningful auditory and vocal experiences, while letter sounds are only a minor aid in pronouncing a momentarily unfamiliar word. To still other authors, learning to read is the process of recognizing written words and sentences drawn almost entirely from the child's own oral language, with minor emphasis upon letter sounds or other approaches to word recognition. Does the average teacher recognize the contradictions among these and other methods? Is she aware of their dependence upon the auditory and visual abilities and experiential backgrounds of

children for their success? Is she aware that no authors of any
system have been able to show that their system was more
effective than others for most pupils exposed to it?

Our obvious point is that methods and materials are often
adopted and used indiscriminately for large masses of pupils.
And, as a result, those pupils who, for any reason, cannot profit
from a system are condemned to failure. Every reading program
in the American market produces a sizeable number of reading
failures when it is used in total class or even large-group
instruction. The proportion of failures, like the average
achievement, may vary greatly from one class to another or, in
other words, from one teacher to the next. But this is a
reflection of differences among teachers...not a reflection of
relative superiority of the method. And, no matter how gifted,
few teachers produce 100% reading success for their pupils,
irrespective of what method they employ. (Spache, 1976,
pp. 120–121)

Teacher Attitude and Reading Disability

Spache (1976) believed that the success or failure of a reading approach
depended more on teacher attitude than on the inherent qualities or
characteristics of specific materials or methods used.

The differences in the success of various systems as measured
by the averages of reading test scores are affected greatly by the
attitude of the teacher toward each system. Some teachers,
welcoming a new approach, enter into its presentation with
great vitality. Others, having doubts or negative feelings about
any new method, grudgingly offer it with little expectation. In
short-term experiments, these contrasting attitudes produce the
kind of reading performances that the individual teacher
expects. She has succeeded in conveying to her students her
feelings about the new approach, and they tend to respond
accordingly. In fact, the teacher manipulates the expectations
and achievements of her class when she is teaching according to
any program, old or new. Even individual children, as well as

the class averages, tend to confirm at the end of the year the
teacher's predictions as made after a few weeks of the term. We
realize, of course, that teachers are not always responsible for
the selection of the reading materials or, hence, the method to
be employed. But we also know that almost any system can be
made reasonably effective if presented enthusiastically.
(pp. 121–122)

The Ultimate Value of Reading Remediation

Although it seems obvious that corrective instruction in reading would have great positive value, Spache raised a number of questions concerning the ultimate outcomes of remediation in reading; questioning these most sacred traditions in reading was typical of Spache throughout his career. As you read, compare Spache's remarks in the following passage (1981) with your own personal experiences in working with students with reading problems. You may not agree with his conclusions, but he raises a number of interesting and disturbing questions.

It may seem paradoxical for me, the author of these texts on
reading disabilities, to question seriously the basic values of
remedial work. On the surface, there appears little justification
for such inquiry, for almost all reports of treatment programs
are optimistic and apparently successful. Moreover, every
worker in the field of remediation can recount happy personal
experiences engendered by the great appreciation shown by
their former students.

But, as we shall see, both these statistical records and the
positive feelings of reading teachers are often founded on very
weak basis. The criteria of gains from treatment are crude and
often give false impressions; the size of the gains considered
significant is given exaggerated emphasis in many instances. To
my knowledge, no one has yet answered the question of what is
"normal" gain for a retarded reader under treatment for a given
period of time. As a result, almost any degree of gain in a post-
training reading test is considered indicative of a successful

treatment program. My review of a sizeable number of reports of gains from treatment supports these criticisms....

Most of us who have been active in remediation of reading disabilities for any sizable period of time are quite certain that such work is fundamentally successful. We see dramatic gains in reading test scores for most of the students we have treated. They are appreciative of our efforts and even years later laud the help they received (Stone, 1967, p. 385). They appear to have more positive attitudes toward reading and to have improved in their self-concepts as readers and students. Moreover, these convictions of the efficacy of redemption are constantly being reinforced by the reports of short-term treatments in our literature.

My purpose in this examination of the outcomes of remediation is to raise the obvious questions that remedial teachers ought to be asking themselves. Such self-probing should query whether there really is evidence of long-term or permanent gain for our students, even for those who perform well in post-training tests. As remedial teachers, we should also be questioning our methods of self-evaluation of our treatments and of predicting the probable outcomes of remedial training under varying conditions. We should be examining our data to discover what influences or factors in remediation are significantly related to the results that we obtain. In fact, it is difficult to see how any teacher or center can intelligently select pupils for remediation without the information about these modifying factors, if they really want to be efficient and to use their resources wisely. (Spache, 1981, pp. 384–385)

Spache (1981) discussed the apparent value of gains in assessment scores from various reading tests as being a valid measure of the inherent effectiveness of remedial reading instruction. The following passage summarizes a much longer and detailed discussion of this topic.

Critics of the reports of what appear to be successful remedial programs point out a number of flaws in the evaluation design as well as in the construction of most of these studies. For example, they see reports of gains for remedial work based on several post-training reading tests that may give contradictory as well as different results.... (p. 385)

What I am trying to point out is that evaluation of short-term remedial reading programs cannot be done accurately by comparison of pretests and posttests, by comparing gains with "normal" growth, or by noting the decrease in the gap in achievement and mental age. There is no good single criterion with which the pretest to posttest gain may be compared.... (p. 387)

In most reports of remedial programs, it appears to be sufficient to convince the editor of the publication, the writer, and some of the readers by finding a statistically significant difference in the pre–posttest gains. If such gains are present, it is supposed to show the validity of the procedures used, as well as the overall effectiveness of the program and the teacher. Yet, we really have very little idea of what degree or amount of gains that remedial work, in contrast with ordinary classroom instruction, should produce in a given time. Is every program that produces almost any gain greater than "normal" maximally effective? Or should we expect remediation to produce twice or three or x times the normal growth?... (p. 389)

About the only sound conclusion we may derive from this review of gains from remediation is that we now have a rough criterion for judging the success of these programs. This conclusion may serve to temper the enthusiastic claims of many who report on their particular programs, by this crude comparison between pre- and post-training. (p. 391)

Long-Term Outcomes of Remediation

In the following passage, Spache (1981) discusses what he believed research said about the lasting effects of remediation in reading. To say the least, he was very negative about these results. Spache also summarizes what he believed should be done if remediation is to be effective.

I have referred frequently to the findings of follow-up studies of the eventual outcomes of remedial treatments. Some remedial workers are quite certain of the positive nature of these results, while others wonder whether they have really affected the child's future. Part of these doubts may be attributed to the conclusions resulting from various ways of evaluating the long-term results. Some, simply ignoring the socioeconomic status of their subjects, claim success because such pupils persist in school or even go to college and may achieve white-collar employment status. They assume that such accomplishments imply quite adequate reading skills when, of course, they prove nothing about the present reading ability of their previous clients. Few studies try to establish the current reading status of pupils who have been treated a number of years earlier, depending rather upon questionnaires, correspondence, and telephone interviews. Other researchers try to ascertain the extent of dropouts and nonpromotions, grades, present school status, student reaction to the treatment program, and incidence of adjustment problems among their former pupils, often without comparing these with the statistics for the appropriate social-class segment of the population. I am inclined to believe that, with the exception of an actual reading test result, these supposed indications of successful treatment are often not very meaningful. Many very poor readers graduate from high school and college and find employment commensurate with those educational qualifications by compensating for their poor reading and through the support engendered by their socioeconomic background, thus proving their motivation rather than their adequacy in reading. In any event, I shall try to summarize these follow-up studies to enable the reader to make his or her own judgments of their validity and meaningfulness.

The interpretation of these results is not simple and direct. Improvements attributed to the treatment in some studies are not present in others, or are shown to be just similar to the general population. This is true for the citations regarding high school graduation, college attendance, employment status, and even grades. When compared with the general population or the control groups who were not treated for their retardation, treated poor readers apparently do not differ greatly in these traits. When reading tests are administered as part of a long-range follow-up, most studies indicate no continued growth after treatment or at least less than normal development. Only five indicate that treated retarded readers are presently functioning at levels normal for age-grade status, on the average.

Considering only these two areas of progress for the moment, we might draw such conclusions as these:

Remedial treatment apparently does not affect school progress appreciably over time. If sufficiently motivated—and provided socioeconomic support and educational opportunities—these pupils succeed about as well as untreated poor readers or the general population. Some may improve their grades above the levels prior to the treatment, to a level sufficient for graduation eventually; but so do untreated poor readers, it would seem, if they are motivated for school success. The bulk of the follow-up studies indicate little or no further development of reading ability anything like the accelerated rate during treatment. After treatment, reading growth tends to revert to the less than normal ratio characteristic of most cases prior to their treatment. Eventual reading performances are poor for age-grade status in most studies.... (Spache, 1981, pp. 396–397)

If long-term results in either reading development or in life or school adjustment are not significant, can we justify remedial reading? In view of these results cited, perhaps the only generalization I can make is that remedial reading with or without counseling or other techniques is symptomatic treatment. It relieves temporarily the reading difficulty but produces, as far as I can discover, no long-range effects. In many respects, remediation of reading difficulties resembles the medical approach to treatment of the common cold. Since the exact cause of the cold is unknown, or at best can only be described as viral or nonviral, treatment is intended only to relieve the annoying symptoms and to prevent the progress of the infection (?) into more complicated ailments.

We remedial workers, too, often cannot establish why a reading disability appears in a student, although we know many factors that could have contributed. We are handicapped in treating the causes, such as intelligence, previous instruction, socioeconomic status, parental attitudes, and personality maladjustment of the pupil. Therefore, like the general medical practitioner, we treat the symptom and give temporary relief to our client. His reading performances usually improve, and he resumes the struggle to compete in the classroom under somewhat more favorable circumstances. Like the medical treatment for colds, remedial reading is palliative, supportive, and, perhaps, preventive, not curative. If my simile is accurate, there is as much justification for remedial reading as there is for treatment of the common cold.

If we make our services constantly available, like the physician, we may expect our pupils to return to us from time to time, particularly during periods when their reading difficulties are disturbing or at crucial transitional periods as in moving from elementary to junior high, to senior high, and to college. Like the medical profession, we should probably be promoting annual check-ups to reassess our students' progress, to anticipate recurring reading difficulties, and to provide supportive treatment. We may never be able to change the pattern of reading problems for many cases, but we certainly can help make school life more tolerable for many by maintaining our helping relationship.

In summary, these conclusions may be pertinent to the organization of our remedial services and may act as guiding principles.

   1. In estimating the probable duration of treatment, expect about twice normal growth for most cases. Progress may be less for those handicapped by socioeconomic status, language difference, emotional problems, or low intelligence.

2. *If a pupil evidences problems of personality maladjustment, consider the use of psychological or counseling techniques as preferable to skill instruction, at least during the early stages of the program.*

3. *Use small-group (four to six) instruction as most effective and economical use of staff time.*

4. *If waiting list is excessive, consider selecting pupils with highest initial status, whether primary or secondary, to shorten treatment time, to produce the desired degree of improvement sooner, and, in the long run, thus to serve more pupils.*

5. *For primary pupils, plan relatively short-term treatments since degree of retardation is not so great as with older pupils. If ratio of improvement to duration of treatment is as great as expected, a favorable reading status may be obtained more quickly in these cases.*

6. *Maintain contact with former cases over the years to check progress, to offer resumption of treatment.*

7. *Terminate treatment when pupil demonstrates reasonable facility with ordinary classroom texts, as in open-book, silent reading tasks. Do not expect him to equal his mental age necessarily, or to perform precisely at grade level in a reading test. At primary grades, a few months' difference is insignificant; at intermediate grades allow about a year's variation; and two to three years at secondary levels in comparing post-treatment reading test with his grade placement. Remember that the middle 50% of the average class does not test exactly at grade placement but tends to vary these amounts from that hypothetical criterion.*

8. *Do not expect dramatic changes in grades or grade point averages. Such gains as do appear may not be obvious until at least six months to a year after treatment.*

9. *Unless parental and student aspirations for academic achievement are high or are increased by the treatment, do not expect remediation to prevent all dropouts.*

10. *If personality or school maladjustments are affecting the pupil's progress, do not expect ordinary remedial instruction to cure all these problems too. It may strengthen self-concept and alleviate some of the minor adjustment problems, but it is not a panacea for emotionally disturbed, poor readers.*

11. *If you emphasize skill development in remedial work, recognize it as a temporary, supportive effort to help the student deal with his current academic problems, not as a cure or even a preventative for future problems. The student's school career may well continue to be hindered by some of the factors that contributed to his present retardation, factors which, perhaps, you cannot alleviate but rather can help him to compensate for from time to time as he needs such assistance. (Spache, 1981, pp. 401–403)*

REFERENCES

Spache, G.D. (1953). A new readability formula for primary grade reading materials. *The Elementary School Journal, 53*, 410–413.

Spache, G.D. (1976). *Investigating the issues of reading disabilities.* Boston: Allyn & Bacon.

Spache, G.D. (1980). *Diagnostic reading scales.* Monterey, CA: California Test Bureau.

Spache, G.D. (1981). *Diagnosing and correcting reading disabilities* (2nd ed.). Boston: Allyn & Bacon.

Stone, E.W. (1967). A follow-up study of off-campus students who attended the University of Florida Reading Laboratory and Clinic. In G.D. Spache (1981), *Diagnosing and correcting reading disabilities* (2nd ed.). Boston: Allyn & Bacon.

Reflections

George Spache took a strong stand on a number of issues related to reading instruction. The following questions are designed to stimulate your thinking about his writing:

1. What are Spache's beliefs about how a teacher's philosophy of reading relates to the ways in which he or she teaches? How does your philosophy of teaching reading compare with that of Spache?

2. Do you agree or disagree with what Spache believed were major problems associated with reading remediation? Compare that to the ways in which you approach reading remediation in the classroom.

FURTHER READING

Spache, G.D. (1976). *Investigating the issues of reading disabilities*. Boston: Allyn & Bacon.
> This is an in-depth study of the many controversial issues related to the field of reading disabilities, such as visual perception, intelligence, and social-cultural factors. Of particular interest is a discussion about a variety of innovative approaches to corrective reading instruction.

Spache, G.D. (1981). *Diagnosing and correcting reading disabilities* (2nd ed.). Boston: Allyn & Bacon.
> In this book, Spache discusses his controversial views about the value of reading remediation, noting that these procedures sometimes may not be worth the effort. Whether you agree or disagree with Spache's basic conclusions, this book is well worth reading.

CONCLUSION

The reading of all good books is like conversation with the finest men of past centuries.

—Rene Descartes

Have you ever rightly considered what the mere ability to read means? That it is the key which admits us to the whole world of thought and fancy and imagination. To the company of saint and sage, of the wisest and the wittiest at their wisest and wittiest moment. That it enables us to see with the keenest eyes, hear with the finest ears, and listen to the sweetest voices of all times.

—James Russell Lowell

Reading is to the mind what exercise is to the body. As by the one, health is preserved, strengthened, and invigorated; by the other virtue (which is the health of the mind) is kept alive, cherished, and confirmed.

—Sir Richard Steele

In anything fit to be called by the name of reading, the process itself should be absorbing and voluptuous; we should gloat over a book, be rapt clean out of ourselves.

—Robert Louis Stevenson

*W*hat can today's classroom teachers learn about reading from their colleagues of the past? Are we so removed from these educators, in both time and teaching conditions, that there is no chance for meaningful dialogue? Have we as reading teachers progressed so far in our current reading practices that we no longer need to consider the thoughts and observations of earlier teachers? These are difficult questions, yet important ones, for teachers to consider as we look to the future.

Often a classic's greatest value is its ability to challenge current thinking about problems and issues—in this case the effective teaching of reading. Reading education has often resembled a pendulum swinging from one extreme to another. What was learned in the past about the strengths and weaknesses of a particular approach or philosophy of reading is seemingly forgotten yet is often reinvented by succeeding generations of educators. Frequently, what is considered new and innovative is often a reworking of ideas and methods of the past. To ignore reading educators of the past is to miss a wealth of valuable insight and perception. Moreover, it results in a limited perspective or provincial view of current beliefs instead of a professional awareness in which the past informs the present (Robinson, Baker, & Clegg, 1998).

General Conclusions

Although there is wide variety in the descriptions of past reading programs and practices, careful reading of these historical documents reveals a consistency in themes. Commonalties recommended by most of the past educators include the following:

- Teaching reading as a lifelong process;
- Developing reading as a thinking process rather than as simply an isolated skill;
- Recommending that each teacher develop an effective definition of the reading process;
- Noting there is no one method or set of materials that is always successful with every reader;
- Treating the results of reading assessment, particularly the outcomes of standardized tests, as being only one indicator of ability or disability;
- Building appropriate background as the foundation for effective reading instruction;
- Identifying reading disabilities as early as possible in a student's educational experience;
- Seeing the importance of reading not as a subject in and of itself, but rather as a tool for learning across the curriculum;
- Describing phonics as only one aspect of word identification in an effective reading program;
- Suggesting the reading of a wide variety of literature;
- Discussing the appropriate role of oral reading;

- Emphasizing the role of the classroom teacher as being paramount in the effective teaching of reading; and perhaps most important of all,

- Encouraging the love of reading in all students.

Suggestions for Further Study

This book provides but a brief overview of the available writing in the field of reading education. I hope that it encourages further investigation of the rich legacy of past thinking and work in this area. An excellent place to find further reading on these topics is the Reading Hall of Fame (IRA, 1996) (http://www.reading.org/dir/ex/hallfame), which lists noted reading authorities.

May your knowledge of these past reading educators inspire you to encourage your students to see reading as did the English writer John Langford, who said,

The love of reading is a love that requires neither justification, apology, or defense.

REFERENCES

International Reading Association. (1996). *Reading Hall of Fame* [Online]. Available: http://www.reading.org/dir/ex/hallfame [2001, September 28].

Robinson, R.D., Baker, E., & Clegg, L. (1998). Literacy and the pendulum of change: Lessons for the 21st century. *Peabody Journal of Education, 73,* 15–30.